Bent Not Broken

Crossing Life's Bridges of
Tragedy, Trauma and Triumph

Landis Graden

Strategic Book Publishing and Rights Co.

Strategic Book Publishing and Rights Co., LLC
USA | Singapore
www.sbpra.net

For information about special discounts for bulk purchases, please
contact Strategic Book Publishing and Rights Co. Special Sales, at
bookorder@sbpra.net.

ISBN: 978-1-68235-388-2

Book Design: Suzanne Kelly

To Riley and Caleb,
May you always live inside your true selves.

TABLE OF CONTENTS

Landis Graden

PREFACE

It was a typical sunny and humid summer day in Washington, DC. I finished lunch and stepped out of the W Hotel for my 1 p.m. meeting. Dressed in my new navy-blue Armani suit, I looked every bit the part of a powerful and successful player. I wanted people to see me and wonder "Who is that? Where is he going?" because I had fought so hard for a day like this to arrive.

After a mere two-minute walk, I was at my destination: 1600 Pennsylvania Avenue. I was a VIP guest, alongside other leading social entrepreneurs and innovators who were invited to discuss social and economic impact in local communities. The goal of the meeting was to tap our collective brains and expand social innovation across the country. We needed to reach more people in need. It was an ambitious agenda, but in my mind, all I could think was that I had arrived.

Adding to my excitement was the fact that I had been invited to the White House at a time when President Barack Obama, the nation's first Black president, occupied it. Like him, I knew what it was like to be raised predominantly by a strong mother. Like him, I had spent a lifetime trying to unravel a complicated relationship with a father I desperately wanted to understand. And like him, I was here as a result of hard work, despite the odds.

I was wanted in this room. I was founder and CEO of a successful public benefit company and the leading social entrepreneurial real estate development firm in California. Our specialty was working with mission-based entities such as governments, school districts, and faith-based organizations. This was a gathering of some of the best and brightest social entrepreneurial minds in our country, and I was among them. I admit: my chest puffed, and my head swelled, something that's difficult to prevent when you find yourself in such a unique position, especially given where I'd come from.

Secret Service moved us swiftly through the line after we showed our IDs. They had already cleared our background checks weeks before. Once inside, we were pointed in the direction of our meeting room and left on our own to find our way. It tripped me out a bit when I learned that once inside the complex we were free to move about without escort. I roamed the rooms of the White House, staring at the portrait of Abraham Lincoln in the State Dining Room. I imagined him in these very rooms, issuing the Emancipation Proclamation. I took extra time to absorb the history and grandeur of the residence. Finally, I moved onto the Eisenhower Executive Office Building next to the West Wing where our meeting was taking place.

I took my seat and gazed at the video screen in front of the room. On it was the seal of the president of the United States of America. I looked around the room at all the entrepreneurs and leaders who had come from all around the country and as I sat there something inside me began to shift. My puffed chest began to deflate. My feelings of confidence, pride, and anticipation were giving way to fear, anxiety, and panic. I felt like an imposter.

This was a mistake, I thought. I did not belong here.

***

There are moments in my life when the person inside me does not match up with the person outside and a conflict ensues. Sitting in a room just yards away from the West Wing was the moment I became aware of my mask, the one I had unknowingly been hiding behind for my entire adult life. The invisible mask that I had created and used to protect myself when I was a child. Now, as a man, it had a paralyzing hold on me. This mask kept me in a place of fear and self-doubt, even at the height of my professional career and even at the White House as a VIP guest sitting inside the seat of power.

It happened slowly, over time, without me even realizing it. But up until that moment in that fateful gathering, I was a person stuck in a chaotic and dysfunctional cycle, surrounded by other stuck people. Together we kept each other submerged in emotional quicksand, always struggling to catch our breaths. We were always in danger of getting pulled under; we were never liberated from the struggle. As I sat there, I began to see that my mind was still operating from the same level of turmoil and dysfunction, trauma, and self-defeating imaginations that it had when I was a kid; that concerned me. My earliest memory of being emotionally and mentally injured is at five years old. I further recalled years of sexual abuse from my female baby-sitter a few years later only to come full circle as a womanizer and cheater later into adulthood. My mind had created tools to help me survive all the trauma no young boy should ever have to endure, and the injury continued well into my teenage years. But as an adult, these survival mechanisms only kept me locked inside that trauma. The worst part of it all was that I was totally unaware that I was being led around the world by the five-year-old boy prominently tucked inside my soul.

The soul never forgets, it only expands or contracts. Our soul hosts within it the sum total of our existence whether we like the memories or not. I remember as a young boy being fascinated by space travel. I watched images of a rocket being launched into space on our old television set. I wondered how the vessel would reach its destination so far from its starting point. Of course, there was a plan for it, and every measure was taken to have that plan carried through. But how do you prepare for the unknown? I equated my birth with the rocket being launched into orbit: all systems were good to go, and my destination was set, but somewhere along the way, a meteor struck and I was taken off course. Then another, and another, until I was so off course that I wondered if I would ever find my way back again.

Meteors are debris from larger objects that have broken off. They serve no useful purpose and are going nowhere fast. They are also prone to collide into perfectly good things like satellites and rockets. I liken people who hurt other people as broken fragments colliding into perfectly healthy people. Once part of a healthy whole, their broken pieces keep moving forward, smashing into other people, breaking off pieces of their whole selves, and so on, and so on. At a certain point, I had to ask myself who the meteors had been in my life. What collisions with them had forced me into another direction? At what point in the journey did I decide to become someone I wasn't destined and designed to be?

A VIP guest at the White House. Dressed in a designer suit. This was the moment that I had to reconcile the mask—the man of success—with the person in turmoil who hid behind it.

And it was this very day that I made the decision to finally take off the mask.

PART 1

"It is easier to build strong children than to repair broken men."

—Frederick Douglass

CHAPTER 1

Ours was an active-duty Navy family, and we moved a lot. I remember how old I was based on where we were living at the time. I was five years old when we lived in Chula Vista in San Diego. Chula Vista was all sunny skies and long stretches of warm sand, with the Pacific Ocean for a swimming pool at nearby Coronado Beach. This was an ideal place for anyone to grow up, but not me. Despite my youth and potential to learn, it was around this time that I first began seeing what my father saw in me: someone who didn't measure up to his expectations. Even though I saw him as a strong powerful figure and looked up to him, my vision of who I wanted him to be was different than my reality. My mom was a beautiful loving woman and my sister was a happy toddler. On the outside, we looked like the perfect happy family and I wanted for us to live up to that billing, but that wasn't to be in this lifetime.

As much as I wanted our family to be perfect on the inside as much as it looked on the outside, one night reminds me of the elusive fantasy that was never to be. I recall a particular evening sitting at the dinner table with my dad. He was one of those "You better clean your plate" type of men. I still had a little food on my plate and had no room in my stomach for more. It didn't help that I wasn't very fond of black-eyed peas at the time either. I tried to finish but was at a point where I couldn't eat another bite. It became a standoff between him and me.

He began yelling at me to clean my plate, while I was trying to convince him I was full and couldn't stomach any more. I assume he thought I was lying because he wouldn't let up. He just kept barking out commands. Out of fear of being punished, I force-fed myself the rest of my food. He was satisfied and felt victorious because his orders were followed. I was miserable,

3

because my stomach was aching and felt like it would burst at any second. Within minutes, and before we both could get up from the table, I threw up all over him. As punishment, I was forced to go to bed long before bedtime and had to confine myself to my room the rest of the night. This was my idyllic San Diego life—the start of an ongoing tug-of-war with my father. He wanted to shape me into something I wasn't. I tried to understand with my five-year-old mind why I wasn't enough. The first layer of disconnect from my emotions was birthed.

A year later, we relocated to Murphy Canyon Lincoln Military Housing in San Diego. This put me in the direct path of an older kid in the neighborhood who took pleasure in bullying me. I was in the first grade. The bully was several grades higher than I—not to mention much larger and taller. Other than being white, I cannot recall any other details about him. Naturally, I was scared. He chased me home every day from school, trying to catch me, but I was always one step ahead. If he did, he'd beat me up. When my father found out about this, he was filled with rage—not toward the boy who was beating his child, but toward me for running. I never did find out how my father found out. I can only assume he saw the kid chasing me home one day.

As was his personality, we didn't talk about it, he just took his own unilateral action that left me without understanding. He was determined to toughen me up. After school one day, he asked me to go in the backyard to dig up clay and fill a pillow-case he handed me. This was the same clay that Native Americans made pottery from, so it was hard and dense. We went into the garage. He tied a rope around the top of the pillowcase and hung it from a rafter. The pillowcase hung there like a punching bag in a boxing gym.

He taped my knuckles. He had me stand in front of the bag. He stood behind it, bracing it like a boxing trainer. Only, he held the makeshift punching bag with one hand and held a belt in the other. He'd yell at me to punch hard. I'd punch with all of my small might. Whenever I failed to hit hard enough to meet his approval, he'd strike me with the belt. He yelled and yelled, and I punched and punched. This turned into a daily routine. In the end, nothing changed. It was a failed experiment. It didn't teach me courage or how to fight. I wasn't suddenly skilled to take on this bully. Punching a bag of clay did little to build my confidence. All he had accomplished was to teach me to fear him. So, now I feared two bullies.

When I was in second grade, I joined the football team, thinking I might be able to please him. I thought if I was good, he would see that I wasn't just a scared boy. After all, football is an all-contact sport. I would be able to prove to him that I could be aggressive. I knew a little about the sport by watching the San Diego Chargers on TV with my dad. Players Dan Fouts and Charlie Joyner were very popular. My mom loved the Oakland Raiders who had Kenny Stabler, Fred Biletnikoff and Jack Tatum. Leading up to our first practice he would excitedly give me tips and pointers. It felt like magic being able to connect with him. I thought finally my fantasy of having the perfect family on the inside was starting to come true.

My dad joined the team too, as an assistant coach. At one of the very first practices in my first football season, another first-year beginner team joined us to scrimmage. Both teams were a collection of seven-year-old scrawny kids being introduced to the sport for the first time. Even though we had all just started the season, the other team had better coaches, and they were a little more advanced than my team. To see how well we were learning, they had us scrimmage.

We weren't keeping score, but if we were, it would've been a blowout. As my team failed to score and tackle, my dad became agitated and frustrated. As was his personality, he always lost to his inner demons even when he didn't want to. One minute he was on the sideline coaching us, screaming and yelling. The next minute he was overcome with his customary rage, furiously walking off the field. I felt torn. We weren't doing well, but we were having fun and learning. Before I knew it, he had abandoned me and the rest of the team on the field. I remember watching him walk away. It took me a minute to realize he wasn't coming back. Although this was the first time, it surely wasn't going to be the last. When it finally hit me that I was abandoned, I became instantly afraid. I looked around at the other dads and coaches who had all stayed. I felt wrong and embarrassed, like I didn't belong. I was confused and felt that I had done something bad. Before his explosion, I was actually having a really good time playing. Although the team wasn't great, I was pretty good and was receiving praise from the coaches. All the coaches had positive comments about my play that day. All except the one that mattered the most, my dad. Where was my dad? Why did he leave me? This was the beginning of what would be a lifelong pattern of his. He was a meteor. Colliding into me.

Back at home later that night, I was summoned to my parents' bedroom. When I opened the door, I saw a worried look on my mother's face. My father's anger had not subsided from the time he left my football practice. Now, he was doubling down. I stood in the doorway of his room. He yelled at me about how terrible our second-grade team was. He scolded me that he was too good to be associated with a bunch of losers, that he would not tolerate being embarrassed. On and on, for what seemed like hours. Instead of giving me a pep talk to boost my confidence, he robbed me of the little bit of hope, confidence, and spirit I had left. He didn't take the time to separate the performance from the performer. It didn't occur to him to provide constructive critique and helpful tips. It didn't dawn on him that his role in that moment was to be my leader, my champion, my guide. He was consumed with his rage and negative emotions without a thought to how this all was impacting me. He didn't think of the toll that the events from earlier that day had on me. He was a meteor. Colliding into me.

Of all the things that happened before and after, this was the incident that broke me. It left me feeling alone, abandoned, helpless, and hopeless. What was supposed to be an awesome learning and growth experience instead turned into a different type of life lesson. Instead of living within the framework of an American dream of father coaching son in football, it became a living nightmare. What I did learn was that no matter how much I tried, it would never be good enough to earn his love and presence. This was the moment when, to protect myself from the psychological abuse, I constructed a mask to hide behind. Another layer of emotional disconnect formed on top of the earlier layers.

When I was growing up, I didn't know what imposter syndrome was. No one talked openly about trauma and abuse. I never talked about what happened to me in my home, because I knew no one would believe or understand me. Being a young black man only further complicated things. My father's approach to making me strong was to make me believe I was weak, and so I had to pretend. Pretend things were okay. Pretend I was not afraid. Pretend I could punch a bag filled with clay as if it didn't hurt. This was the mask I created to be, at least on the outside, who I thought people expected me to be. But all I was doing was becoming part of a pattern—a pattern that began long before I was even born.

CHAPTER 2

I never knew much about my great-grandparents. I'm almost certain, though, that if I could go back and look at generation after generation, I would uncover patterns of abuse. I would expose pain, neglect, and falsehoods, like deep, aged roots so intricately intertwined they are impossible to unravel. These are the roots I came from, and if I ever wanted to grow in a different direction, I would have to find a way to loosen those bound roots. I had to avoid the entanglement of the past and the grip of the status quo. This required a lot of introspection, a lot of researching about my family, and a lot of studying patterns of human behavior. One of the most difficult aspects of being introspective was the willingness to confront the truth, no matter how ugly, and be honest about how I was falsely projecting myself to the world. I needed to unlearn some old habits to reveal the real me.

Ever since I discovered my stuck thinking, I've been in search of understanding how my mind was programmed, so that I could reprogram it to unstick it. I wanted to learn about emotional needs and wants. I wanted to learn about why I was lacking empathy. I wanted to understand why I would choose unhealthy ways to solve problems. I wanted to learn about my father's story and how legacy impacted the present. I wanted to understand why some people were able to maintain discipline while others lacked it. Most of all, I wanted to know why I acted and thought and behaved the way I had, so I could live a life of truth, purpose, and passion. I was preoccupied with the question: "Why do people keep bad habits that they know aren't good for them?" I came across two tidbits of information in my early investigation into breaking patterns of abuse that demonstrate how this works.

Residents of Massachusetts spend on average $737.01 on lottery tickets per year. There is a 1 in 292,201,338 chance of winning Powerball, and a 1 in 302,575,350 chance of winning Mega Millions. If that person invested nothing more than what they lost in the lottery every year for 40 years—that's $737.01 per year, or about two bucks a day—at 12 percent interest, he would have $603,716.13 saved just from investing the lottery money. If he added $50 more per month, he would have $1.1 million dollars by the time he was ready to retire.

Here's another one to think about: if you were to read ten books per year for five years on a single subject—any subject—you would have so much knowledge on that subject that you would be considered a world expert.

What I learned from these two examples is that once a habit is formed, it takes on a life of its own, even if it doesn't make sense. It becomes encoded in the subconscious and runs on an endless loop. The loop becomes its own ecosystem, and no matter how much I want to form a new habit, the old habit sticks. Relying solely on my conscious mind to change the habit I wanted shifted was not enough. I needed to reboot and reprogram the entire hard drive that would ultimately change my thought patterns. I hypothesized if I could change my thinking, I could change my behaviors with positive, life-giving habits that would change my life.

Instead of hoping to win it big by playing the lottery, I could do the hard work of saving and investing. Instead of wishing I were smarter or better at something, I could do the hard work of reading books and learning how to become an expert. But in order to get there, I needed to change my hoping and wishing to believing that I could actually do it. And in order to do that, I needed to understand why I thought that way in the first place. I needed to understand why "doing things the way they've always been done" was considered normal and that in continuing with that status quo kept me stuck chasing mediocrity. If all it took was for me to invest a little bit of money every month to become a millionaire, then why hadn't I started much sooner in life? Or if I wanted to be at the top of my game in my profession, and

I had all the books already at my disposal, then why wasn't I reading them?

Why didn't I realize I was capable of overcoming, persevering, and thriving? No matter where I came from, no matter what I've been through, and no matter how hard life had been during my youth, wasn't positive change available to everyone? I knew it was possible, but I also knew I needed to confront impostor syndrome and dig deep into my subconscious. In order to unleash the power of my potential, I needed to release the weights and scars that had held me back for so many years. To discover the purpose for my life, to live within my truth and find my destiny, I had to identify what I had been taught, unlearn the bad stuff, and invest in new ways of thinking. I had to uncover the patterns that I had internalized if I ever hoped to find freedom.

The mask I put on in the doorway of my father's room at five years old had one job: to protect me from harm by shielding my emotions, especially from my father. As I grew up, the mask grew with me, from a coat of armor to protect the emotions of a child, to an elaborate illusion to protect the ego of a man. What I looked like to the outside world was a successful, together man, while on the inside I felt constant turmoil. I did nothing to address that turmoil, and instead invested everything in my outward appearance and material success to make sure people perceived me in a specific way. I had learned how to do it so long ago, and had done it so well for so long, that I didn't even realize I didn't have to live like this. I didn't know I had a choice.

I, like everyone else, was a product of my relationships, environment, customs, and culture. Before I was born, I consumed sounds, emotions, and chemicals. From inside my mother's womb, I was exposed to whatever she was exposed to. Whatever she ate or drank, I ate and drank. When she felt stress, I felt stress. There was a single symbiotic existence between us. As babies, we have no control over what gets deposited into us, but those deposits serve us, whether good or bad, and they don't stop in utero. They continue on as our parents and guardians shape us in their likeness as we develop.

That likeness is omnipotent and molds us in ways that it is nearly impossible to change. If we are taught that the perfect life is to go to college, get a job, get married, buy a house, have children, and wait for the grandchildren, chances are we'll do our best to do those things and we'll never question why. They'll be automatic ambitions given to us before we even know how to dream for ourselves, and that's when certain of us experience confusion and anguish. When we start dreaming and those dreams do not match our grooming, there is a disconnect that also invites discontent. Chances are, after long, many of us will end up unhappy or unfulfilled. Problems manifest when we start to wonder why. After all, we've done what we were told to do, so where is our peace and treasure?

Before we take charge of the way we show up in the world, we are curated by others. I've watched my children play and have fun no matter the race, color, or gender of their playmates. I've also watched over the years how certain children decide it's no longer fun to play with children that do not look like them. Somewhere between innocence and awareness, at some point, these children were taught to hate, and what was once innocent play with childhood friends was replaced with discrimination against race, gender, religion, classism, or some other bias. They began reliving handed-down patterns. The mind they had that was once open and boundless is now filled with division. How do we know what thoughts, values, and behaviors are *really* ours versus behavioral patterns we are merely perpetuating?

You start at the root.

CHAPTER 3

L aurens is a rural town in northwestern South Carolina. The town was built around its historic Court House Square. A railroad expansion in the late nineteenth century led to the town's growth, paving the way for it to become a major trading center focused on cotton crops and production, as well as textile, manufacturing, and glass. My father, Landis Vernard Graden, was born here on July 14, 1947, contributing to Laurens County's growth from 37,382 residents in 1900 to 46,974 in 1950. The town was dotted with beautiful Victorian homes with wide patches of green lawns. Stores and businesses with brick facades and old Coca-Cola signs filled the downtown area, giving it an all-American Main Street feel. Like my San Diego surroundings as a child, it was an idyllic backdrop for any child growing up. But not for my father.

This was the Jim Crow south. Racism permeated and infected the tree-lined streets, seeping into homes and into the residents' souls. This outside tension only exacerbated the pressures within my father's childhood home. My dad's father, my grandfather, was an alcoholic and was abusive to my grandmother. My father, along with his two brothers and two sisters, often witnessed both abuses. Of all his siblings, my father was a mama's boy and was the closest of all the children to his mother. He was a shy and obedient boy, but watching his mother being abused from a young age planted a seed of pain that grew into rage as he got older.

I don't have many facts about my father's family of origin and what I was able to piece together from my mother, sister and relatives contains some level of speculation. My grandparents were never married and split when my father was about eight years old. When my grandmother began dating another man and

12

announced that she was expecting, my father had hoped things would start turning around, that maybe my grandmother had finally found happiness and that their family could live in peace with the arrival of a new baby. But that hope was short-lived.

My grandmother died giving birth to a baby boy, Pete. During labor, she lost a lot of blood and was in need of a transfusion, but there was no blood available for her. On her deathbed, she was able to say goodbye to all of the children. But my father was the only one who didn't kiss her. At eleven years old, he was too shy and too embarrassed to kiss his mother in front of everyone. When he went back the next day to give his mother a kiss in private, she had already died. This would haunt him for the rest of his life.

My father and his mother had been inseparable up until then. She was his entire world. The hole her death left in his heart was never filled. In an instant, a moment that was supposed to be so beautiful, turned to sorrow. A moment in which life was entering into the universe also delivered death. On that delivery table, an uncle was born, a mother was gone, and a father was lost.

To the best of our understanding, after my grandmother died, my uncle Pete was given up for adoption. My aunts were sent to live with a relative, and my father and his brothers were sent to live with my grandfather. Not only did the children lose their mother, they also lost each other.

My grandfather's bad habits did not end when he split from my grandmother. He continued his alcoholism and abuse, only now he turned it toward his sons. My father went from being a sweet boy to a bitter one, because he had no one to help him heal. He was left without guidance to mourn in a way that would allow him to flourish and live a life his mother would be proud of. His volatile relationship with my grandfather came to a boiling point when, at sixteen, my father got his hands on a gun. He pulled it on my grandfather after a particularly brutal beating. Although he missed, my father took aim and shot. It sent a message: this would be the last time my father suffered at the hands of my grandfather. He left immediately after, moved to a relative's home in Oakland, California, and briefly attended Chabot College in Hayward before joining the Navy in late 1966.

My father was stationed at the Mare Island Naval Shipyard in Vallejo, California, when he met my mother in 1968. She was still in high school at the time. My mom used to tell me stories about the sweet, charming, and handsome man she met, and I would wonder how that magic got lost along the way. They were married in a shotgun wedding on March 20, 1970, and like many other young black men during that era, my father went to Vietnam and came back an even more broken man. My mother no longer recognized the man she married. This became clear when he told her that no woman deserved to be treated better than his mother. Perhaps it was out of guilt for not being there when his mother died. Maybe it was because he missed the chance to kiss her that one last time as she had requested. Or maybe it was not being able to save her from a life of abuse. Whatever the reason, my father had decided that he had failed his mother, and that he was incapable of the type of love he wished he could have shown her in those final days. So, my father turned to what he had been taught best. He hardened his heart, clenched his fist, and became his father. In doing so, he made my mother a victim just as my grandmother had been, and the pattern continued for another generation.

There was no way that I could have understood this as a child. My father never talked to me about his life before us. I knew that he joined the Navy at a young age and fled the south like so many before him. But the rest remained a mystery until years later, after he died and I went through his belongings. I took each photograph, each article of clothing, each seemingly menial possession, and I treated them as valuable pieces of a puzzle I had been trying to solve my whole life.

Despite the bad, I clung to the good. In many ways, this made our situation even more heartbreaking, because I knew what he was capable of and how different our lives could have been. My father was one of the most intelligent people I ever met. His mind was sharp and complex. He rose to the rank of senior chief, which isn't easy. To be advanced to the rank of senior chief, you have to be committed. Your peers and your master chief must approve of you, with reviews and evaluations that showcase excellence. There are no tests for that rank; it is based purely on how great a leader you are.

My father was all the way woke. He was a very intense man when he locked onto something. He loved to debate and argue, if necessary, and had to be right or he wouldn't stop talking until he convinced you that he was correct, or you just couldn't take it anymore and relented out of mercy for a respite. He loved tinkering with old cars. He was a master welder and worked on nuclear subs. He loved grand gestures and had a great sense of humor. His all-time favorite pastime was golf. He loved to cook Saturday morning breakfast, he loved to listen to blues, and he loved to drink.

Growing up in a military family brought with it a lot of extended relatives. My dad's shipmates were his brothers; their kids were my siblings. The Fourth of July and Memorial Day were always special. I'd get up with my dad at 5 a.m. to reserve a spot at Admiral Baker's Field, a hidden paradise for military families in the area. The mothers socialized, the kids swam, and the dads got drunk on Schlitz and Coors. Dad loved to talk and joke and exaggerate when he was drinking, but most of all he was fun. I never saw my dad lighter and happier than he was on those days we were at the cookout.

If only he could have channeled all that into something positive. He could have been a prosecutor with the type of analytical and strategic mind he had. If only he had felt worthy enough. Instead, he did everything he could to protect his heart out of fear of being hurt. All he succeeded in doing was hurting himself and those who tried to love him. He steeled himself to avoid affection in order to avoid feeling, once again, the pain he felt as a child. The mask he wore hid his feelings of loss, longing, and love, and replaced it with cruelty, detachment, and disdain. This is the false persona he slowly created throughout each stage of his life—as a young child watching his father abuse his mother, as an adolescent losing his mother, and as a young man facing his father's rage. In the end, this is what killed him. It wasn't the massive stroke that did it, his broken heart did.

CHAPTER 4

Annetta Marie Penn, my mother, was born on January 12, 1951, in Galveston, Texas. By that time, the city and port along the southeast coast on Galveston and Pelican Island had reinvented themselves twice. Before the devastating Galveston Hurricane of 1900, the region was a major commercial center with one of the busiest and largest ports in the country. The hurricane was so destructive that to this day it is still regarded as the deadliest natural disaster in the United States. By the time my mother was born, during the Prohibition era, the city was nearing the end of its comeback. Galveston had remade itself into a mecca for illegal gambling. This came to an end in the 1950s, ushering in yet another new economic era of <u>tourism</u>, <u>health care</u>, <u>shipping</u>, and <u>financial</u> industries. As a port city, it had a lot to offer—beautiful beaches, boardwalks, and historical districts—but there was no time for that. My grandparents were focused on their growing brood.

My mother was the middle child of seven siblings. My grandmother, Johnnie Mae Penn, had her eldest child, Edwin Sims, with a man in Chicago. Her second eldest, Treina Penn, was from another man from Galveston, and my mother and her two younger brothers and two younger sisters were from my grandfather, John Penn. He was a career Navy man, having reached the respectable rank of master chief. Unfortunately, this meant he was rarely home. He was often deployed, leaving my grandmother without the support and attention she needed from him as she cared for the children. There is physical abuse, and there is abuse from neglect. In many ways, the latter can be much more painful than the former.

My grandmother filled the void his absence left by totally investing her emotions into her children's well-being. She put aside her own needs and committed herself to theirs. This was something she was used to doing: filling voids and creating coping mechanisms. Growing up in New Orleans, she was left in the care of family members and rarely saw her mother, my great-grandmother. My grandfather, on the other hand, grew up in Kentucky and was the son of a moonshiner. He understood the life of a hustler, being on the go and leaving home as opportunities arose. And so they entered their marriage, one seeking to right a wrong from childhood, the other replicating a life he understood.

My mother's family was a military family, so they moved a lot. They relocated from Galveston to Pensacola, Florida, when she was five years old. In just a matter of months, they would move to San Diego, then to Oakland, and then back to San Diego, where there was some semblance of stability from 1960–66. During this time, my mom was coming into her own and was very active in junior high school and high school. She was a member of the Girl's Club, girl's choir at school, a cheerleader, and she was a leading member of charm school, which is what we call modeling nowadays. She even modeled for JC Penny's during those years. In 1966, my grandfather was transferred to the Mare Island Naval Shipyard in Vallejo, and my mom enrolled in Vallejo Senior High School on Nebraska St. in Vallejo. She was a senior when she met the handsome Navy man stationed at Mare Island, my father. After they married and had children, they led the military life my mother was already so familiar with, moving around as my father's duty stations frequently changed. Her childhood had trained her for this life.

Like my grandmother, my mom was a great support system for her children and was dedicated to us despite her troubled marriage. Because she was very close to her siblings, we grew up with our aunts and uncles actively in our lives. She loved to host daily gatherings, and she always wanted people to have a good time. She kept us involved with sports, band, and other activities to keep us busy. She was a devout Christian, so she made sure our lives always revolved around the church and our faith. But beneath her cheerful, hospitable demeanor was a battered wife. For ten years, she carried the weight of this secret in silence. To this day, with my father being dead almost twenty years, she still hasn't put down all the weight and his ghost is still present.

Growing up, my mom was my rock. She was strong, brave, beautiful and bold. I was in awe of her work ethic and effort to see her family thrive. She always instilled in me and my siblings a strong sense of values, faith, family, and service. I desperately wanted my father's approval, but what kept me going was that I always knew I had my mother's. I clung to her as I imagine my father clung to his mother before she died at such a young age. And as my father had feared for my grandmother's safety and her happiness, I also feared for my mother's each time I would hear my father's voice rise like lava spewing from a volcano. I sometimes wondered why she stayed, but I understood what it felt like to be paralyzed, physically and mentally, by his words, the grip of his gaze, and the sting of his hand. How could I blame her when I understood exactly what she was feeling? We were in the same sinking ship—and it was time to jump.

The end of my parents' marriage was as tumultuous as their relationship. My mom, along with me and my siblings, left the house under police escort. We fled the house abruptly, and I assumed my mom feared for her life. That was all my ten-year-old mind could come up with. We were taken to the house of a shipmate who was as close as family. He and my father served together for years, and our two families were inseparable. His home was ten minutes away in Murphy Canyon, but it felt like an hour ride in the back of that black-and white car. This was my mom's big chance—a new beginning to an old story of love and heartbreak.

We arrived at our temporary sanctuary in a few short minutes, but this place would become my tomb. Even though I was emotionally depleted by now from our family dynamic, my father was still a hero to me, and I had not given up on him. I held tightly to the hope that he'd embrace me once again. I would wait patiently for the protection and love of a father, daydream about him chiseling me into a strong, courageous, and skillful man that could take the world by storm and have it my way. Those fantasies never were far from the front of mind, even when his dysfunctional actions would push them to the back.

On the first night at our new temporary living quarters, I was sent downstairs to sleep on the living room floor. My mother, sister, and brother (who was three) stayed upstairs with our hosts. The night before I was in my childhood bed, and on this night I was on a strange floor in the dark, all alone. I pulled the covers over my head to hide from whatever was lurking in the dark. As soon I drifted off to sleep, all hell broke loose.

My slumber turned into panic as the rear patio glass door in the room where I was sleeping exploded and shards of glass flew everywhere. After a few seconds, I had the courage to peek from under the covers. I surveyed the scene and found a volley-ball-sized boulder resting inches from my head. Although I was buried in glass, I was unhurt and managed to sprint upstairs in a panic, with my feet seemingly never touching the floor. I found my mother, siblings, and hosts all hysterical, hiding together in a bathroom. I found immediate comfort from reuniting with the rest of the clan, and my young ten-year-old mind had no idea what was happening.

And then I heard the words that instantly killed something inside me, taking my sense of security, identity, and trust: "Graden is trying to kill us."

Us? I thought. *My father wants me dead?* I was already wrestling with the thought of him wanting to harm my mother, but his own children were also targets; it was just too much. I couldn't reason it, but I accepted it as true because my protector said so.

That tomb I referred to was my instant fear and paranoia that would redefine how I viewed and understood my father. The adults failed me in that moment. They didn't protect my young, fragile spirit. They instead took my father from me. I now saw him as the enemy that at first opportunity would slit my throat. I went from being a wanting little boy, always holding onto hope to spend time with him, to being terrified of him. Not only that,

19

I lost my ability to trust people, something I wouldn't regain until I was in my forties. Here in the middle of this soul killing moment, another layer of disconnect was piled on. In just five years, I had gone from an idealistic five-year-old living in Chula Vista to a semi-disconnected ten-year-old losing himself miles at a time, not inches.

There was no discussion before or after that moment. When met with silence, our minds will do what they must to fill in the blanks.

My mother filed the divorce papers after that, on August 22, 1979. Something terrible happened in the summer of 1979—something so bad that, to this day, my mother refuses to speak to anyone about it. My father was deployed overseas in October 1979, and by the time he returned, the marriage was all but dissolved. Even at ten years old, I knew this was an inflection point. Our lives were about to change. No more abuse, no more bullying, no more yelling. What I didn't realize then, was that, for a majority of my life, the scars left behind, the patterns I'd inherited, would follow me no matter where I went.

My mother never remarried after that. I believe it was because she never wanted to be controlled by a man again. I also think she was averse to the fear of failing in a relationship again, so instead of falling in a love with a man in a healthy dynamic, she gave up on it. She took on three jobs to support us in the aftermath of that dramatic day when we fled our home. Despite everything, she remained unwavering in her Christian faith, which she relied on for a number of years before she eventually found her independence. Years later, she started travelling. She set her feet on African and South American soil, among so many other places. She began to take in stray family members, having once been in need of a safe haven herself. When she was already a grandmother, she went back to school and earned her associate's degree from Solano Community College in Fairfield, California, not far from where she attended high school. She earned her bachelor's and master's degrees in Marriage and Family Therapy from St. Mary's College in Moraga, California. She took on volunteering as a counselor, with a special focus on women survivors of domestic violence. She also took on volunteering at church, constantly seeking to help and serve people whose burdens were too heavy for them to carry alone.

But none of this happened overnight. For a while after we left my dad, it looked like we were finally going to be okay, but once again the hopes of a son for his mother were short-lived. And any hopes I had for myself and this new change on the horizon would quickly disintegrate.

PART 2

"There is no greater agony than bearing an untold story inside you."

—Maya Angelou

CHAPTER 5

I was now the boy of the house. Often when no father is present, we'll tell boys that they are the man of the house. This is always a mistake. Being the so-called man of the house doesn't automatically add protection to the family. For me, all it did was put a burden on my shoulders that I was too young to carry. Not only did I feel responsible for myself and my mother, I also had two younger siblings who now looked to me as a surrogate father. I was ten years old.

My sister, Annena, was seven during the great escape, three years younger than me. She was left standing alongside me among the ruins my father left behind. My brother, Anthony, was only three. He was the lucky one—too young to witness the drama between our parents and too innocent to be influenced by my father's abuse. I envied both of them. They still had a chance to be children. I was left questioning whether I was a boy or a man. How could I be their protector when I had been conditioned by my father to feel fear?

The sounds of my mother's screams, cries, and shrieks still reverberated in my mind. They were the sounds of violence that frequently filled our home, especially at night after my siblings and I were put to bed. Annena and I would be jarred awake. We'd each make our way to the top of the stairs where we'd meet. My parents always turned up the music really loud to mask the symphony of violence that was occurring under the rhythm of the music. For my baby sister, she was unaware of what was happening. She recently told me after reading the first draft of this book that she thought they were just partying as was customary. She told me "Landis, I had no idea what was happening, but you knew. You would always take me into your room and put me in your bed and tell me to go to sleep. You

25

absorbed all that trauma to protect me and you never breathed a word about what you heard, saw or experienced." I was in my own personal terror, paralyzed by panic and helpless with no one to soothe my soul but God himself. These traumas more than anything before or after are where I learned to absorb pain, bury it deep down and keep it moving. Layer upon layer of disconnect formed, but what was I to do? I needed to survive and learning not to feel was better than escape, it was survival.

These were unnatural acts committed by a man who was supposed to protect us. Instead, he was destroying us. And now I was expected to succeed where he had failed, but boys are not mature men. They cannot protect their families against attack, whether physical, emotional, or spiritual. How do I know? Because I couldn't even protect myself from what happened next.

After the divorce, my father moved from San Diego to Washington State to work on a nuclear base. We had almost no contact from the time I was in fifth grade all the way until my freshman year in high school. We knew he was alive because he eventually started sending child support. These were extremely difficult years for all of us. My mother was under dire financial pressure. She had three young mouths to feed and was in constant fear that my father would return and try to finish what he started. I remember the first time I saw her completely lose it. She applied for food stamps to help make ends meet because she had been temporarily laid off. Instead of denying her, they gave her twenty-five dollars for a family of four. We were living in a rented four-bedroom house in a middle-class white neighborhood, and social services advised her to move to a two-bedroom apartment in the hood. She told them off and kept fighting for our survival.

I was still afraid of my father, but slowly, my fear began to turn into the familiar longing to have my father in my life to do things that sons and dads did. I was surrounded by friends with intact, functional nuclear families. Every day I was reminded of what we didn't have, and watching my friends relate with their fathers was excruciating. I longed as I watched all the father-son interactions like fishing, playing catch, or coaching their teams and cheering at their games. I felt a relentless aching in my soul. How I wanted that love, attention, and support of a father. But I didn't have it, and the only thing that remained was the feeling that I was unworthy of that love. I thought my life was less valuable than my friends'.

My longing for that kind of relationship with a father preoccupied my entire youth. To soothe myself, I would look back and rewrite history, thinking my father's abuse wasn't so bad; at least it meant he was there. The abuse was at least some form of attention. I was desperate for my dad to be there for me, to love me and show me the way. I was without a leader, a protector, and a champion. The void he left and the damage he created went unchecked. I was consumed by my desire for a relationship with him, but on the outside, as I had learned long ago, I showed none of this heartache. At this tender young age, my priority was to make it through the day. My ego had been shattered, and in its place I doubled down on my mask and built up a false ego to serve as the bridge between me and the outside world. Between sanity and insanity. Without the protection of a father, I was left to protect myself, and that was how I did it. I was young and unskilled in the art of healthy survival. I was merely doing the best I could to keep my head above water.

Fathers serve a very sacred role in the life of their children. This is especially true for sons. They protect us, cover us, and help us find our courage, confidence, and esteem. They are the booming voice and heavy hand needed to push us back on course whenever we drift. Fathers are the foundation of the family and the pillar of the children's ability to learn bravery. If the father fails at this job, everyone suffers. And so we suffered a new kind of pain—the pain of abandonment.

It didn't help those feelings of abandonment that my siblings and I barely saw my mother. Without the financial support of my father, she had to take on three jobs. She worked as a manicurist at a high-end nail salon, a data entry employee at a law firm, and as a model. We became latchkey kids, which meant we'd have babysitters. Our daily babysitter was Monica, a high schooler much older than me and my siblings. She was convenient. She lived across the street. I was in fourth grade, and she was in tenth grade—a typical age of maturity for a babysitter. The only problem was that she was a pedophile. And I was her victim.

She molested me nearly every night. From the time she started babysitting us until the end of my seventh-grade year, she abused me. At first, I had no idea what was happening. I hadn't been through sex education. No one had the conversation about the birds and bees with me. Not too young to be told I was man of the house, but far too young to be given knowledge of my own body. So, without this love and understanding of my body, and how and when to healthfully engage it, another vulnerable part of my innocence was stolen from me.

She would wake me up after I had gone to bed and proceed through the motions of sexual intercourse with me. If I were the man of the house as everyone had been telling me I was, wouldn't I have been able to protect myself from this child molester? Wouldn't I have been able to protect my body? If I really were the man of the house, I would have guarded my soul and stood watch over my future. But it was all a lie. I was not the man of the house. I was only a child who was nothing but an imposter, someone who had constructed an elaborate mask to help me emotionally escape the trauma, or at least hide it away in a dark corner somewhere.

I don't remember many details. I only know I felt numb and indifferent. I do not recall pleasure but I do remember feeling confused. At the time, I didn't know these actions were even called "sex." And I definitely didn't know that, for consenting adults, it could be a beautiful act of love. I didn't know that my young mind needed to grow and mature before I learned about sex. What I did know is what I was told: not to tell anyone about what happened. So, I didn't. Since I had already been wearing masks and had learned to bury trauma inside my heart out of view of the world, being silent about my abuse was something I did rather effortlessly. Even now thinking about my fourth grade self who by such a tender age had developed nerves of steel and a nonchalant attitude about sexual abuse speaks volumes about just how broken I was emotionally and spiritually by this point in life. The abuse and the silence, to this day, I can't measure the damage they caused. I can still feel the pull of that trauma from time to time, a few hard wires in my brain disconnecting. It took a long time to realize how the damage had wired my thinking, how it impacted the way I would grow to treat, and mistreat, women . . . how being who the meteor had crashed into would turn me into another meteor hurtling blindly through space.

Despite what she took from me, I never betrayed my abuser's trust. I only just told my mother a couple years ago, nearly forty years after the fact. Abuse and the trauma and damage it leaves is complicated, and many of us find ourselves in the position of protecting the ones who should have been protecting us. I have wondered many times what made Monica commit such a heinous act on a child. But knowing what I know now, I can only believe that she must have been in pain. She must have been, at some point, like me. Someone inflicted their pain upon her, and now her pain was inflicted onto me. That pain stretched into my future and created an unhealthy dynamic that I would have with women and sex for much of my adult life.

I can only assume she found validation and escape through sex. Perhaps she was also sexually molested as a child and knew nothing more than to perpetuate it. Considering how I was impacted, it's not too far of a stretch to recognize the dynamic. Someone possesses our body and at the same time penetrates our soul and our emotional brain, leaving in its wake a certain brokenness that never really fully heals. The wound is always deep inside and can be placed in a state of dormancy, out of reach to sow further dysfunction.

Throughout those years of abuse, I learned the art and tactics of advanced survival. Out of necessity and a desire to live as normal as possible, I became a master at creating a facade. From the outside, I was a well-adjusted kid. By the time I was thirteen, I was earning all A's in school and excelling at football and baseball. I was popular in the neighborhood and at school.

29

I had become so good at faking it that I even fooled myself into thinking I was happy. And then we got the call.

My maternal grandfather was gravely ill. My mother, wanting to spend his last days with him, decided we would move into my grandparents' home in the San Francisco Bay area. Though I hated to leave all my friends, the move would finally get me away from my abuser. We'd also be able to save some money, so maybe my mom wouldn't have to work so much. We could spend more time with her. Being around my grandfather would give me a positive male role model, and being around my cousins would give me an identity I longed for. This was my hope. So we headed north, and in my mind we had another chance to press the restart button.

CHAPTER 6

In the summer of 1983, millions of people watched on their television sets as NASA launched its eighth mission and the third flight of the space shuttle *Challenger*. All space travel was fascinating to me, but what was especially significant about this mission was that it was carrying the first Black astronaut, Guion Bluford. I wondered what kind of family he came from—if he had been raised in a happy home with a loving father, or if he had been raised in a home like mine. Was he able to reach this height of success because he was given all the support and guidance he needed as a child? Or did he succeed despite the fact that he had neither? I had hoped it was the latter, because that would mean I had a chance to make something of myself.

I tried to wrap my head around the concept of traveling beyond Earth. I remember watching and wondering how the spacecraft could make it from our planet to its destination and back undamaged. How was it possible to not get consumed by the infinite darkness of space? I sat mesmerized along with the rest of the world as I was navigating my own complicated journey. I hoped that the damage I had sustained would not deter me from where I needed to go—or at least that it would not consume me in its darkness.

This was the same summer we moved into my grandparents' home in Union City, about thirty miles southeast of San Francisco. My grandfather, desperate to spend time with my mother before he passed, was grateful to have us there. He was deployed so often when she was young that he missed much of her childhood. Maybe this was his way of righting a wrong. The home was a four-bedroom, two-bath ranch-style house on Carmen Way. When we got there, everything was perfect. I already knew all the kids in the neighborhood from all the trips there we'd taken over the years on Thanksgiving and Christmas. My mom's entire family lived either in Union City or Oakland. We were no longer alone on an island unto ourselves in San Diego. We were surrounded by family, uncles, aunts, and all my many cousins.

We lived in a middle-class neighborhood. All my friends lived in two-parent homes and had dual incomes. We were the only family in my entire circle of friends whose parents were divorced. Although we lived in this nice home, it was my grandparents' home. We had very little, sometimes no money. We were boarders there, and it felt like it. My mother did her best to provide for our needs but it was tough. My grandparents themselves were on a fixed income and couldn't really help much with the extra mouths to feed.

Despite that struggle, our first year in Union City was a happy one. Being able to spend time with my grandfather before he passed was a gift. He never had much of a formal education, but he was a brilliant man. I would often sit beside him in the living room as we both watched television. He never failed to guess the words or phrases on *Wheel of Fortune*, and more often than not, he would ask the right questions on *Jeopardy*. We spent a lot of time talking and watching game shows and just getting to know each other. I will never forget that year.

That summer, I was between seventh and eighth grade. I was in the grips of puberty, and though the surroundings weren't totally new, I still had a lot of settling in to do. I reacquainted with old friends and made lots of new ones. We spent the entire summer just being kids, playing and having fun. When fall rolled around, we enrolled in the local middle school. I joined the sports teams and resumed playing in the school band. For the first time in a long time, I don't remember having a care in the world. I also witnessed another first: I had never, in my entire childhood, seen my mom so happy. I can honestly say, in that year, she was at peace. She was safe and full of joy.

As soon as I started to feel like I could finally be myself, my grandfather lost his battle with emphysema. After the best summer and school year I had ever had—almost exactly twelve months since our arrival in Union City—we lost him. The chain of events that followed would slowly erase all the joy, peace, and happiness we experienced. And in its place, my childhood trauma, which I thought was behind me, would rear its head again, triggered by a new set of challenges.

Prior to our arrival in Union City, two of my mom's brothers weren't doing so well. In fact, they were doing quite badly. Both of them were alcoholics and also addicted to drugs—One to heroin, the other to crack. I later learned that my grandfather had kicked them out of the house in order to make room for us. He felt it was important to provide a safe and secure home for my mother and her children than to provide refuge to his dysfunctional sons. My grandfather had been the only thing standing between them staying away and moving back in. I do want to note that both of my uncles have their own complicated backstories and they were once idyllic boys who like me had a damaging relationship with their own father that sent them spinning off course. So kicking them out of the house to accommodate us probably came very easily to my grandfather but to his sons, it must've been just another note to prove how unimportant they were to him.

So, soon after his funeral, one by one, my grandmother allowed my drug-addicted uncles to return to the home. I was fourteen years old, my sister was eleven, and my brother was seven. It is difficult to explain what it's like living with substance abusers. Violence, crime, abuse—addicts will do anything and everything they can for that next fix. We soon experienced firsthand that horror and trauma, escaping one life of pain only to be thrown into another.

My freshman year began the fall of 1984, and the house was in constant chaos. Our things would go missing, there were constant fist fights, and my uncles' criminal and objectionable people were coming and going, some of whom were drug dealers and drug users. We had become one of the most visited residences by the local police. My mom, once again finding herself engulfed in pure craziness, started to check out emotionally. This time I was a bit closer to manhood, and as such took on the mantle of becoming the literal primary protector of my brother and sister.

One day, I heard my sister with one of my uncles. He had started to harass her. Their voices were raised. Then, he put his hands on her. I ran down the hallway, saw nothing but red, and jumped into protection mode. I tackled him to the ground and put him in a headlock. I was screaming at him, "Never touch my sister again!" I felt pure rage. My grandmother heard all of this from another room and ran over to intervene. I was relieved to see her coming, but in an instant that relief turned to anguish and bitterness as she instead took his side.

I became her target. She started hitting me, telling me to get off of her son. I was doing my best to defend my sister from being abused, and relying on nature, I expected my grandmother to do the same. Instead, she wanted to protect my uncle, who was high and harassing his eleven-year-old niece. Still, I thought she would immediately and unceremoniously kick him out. Instead, her ire turned to us; she wanted us gone.

By this point in my life, I watched my father physically abuse my mother and then abandon me. I had been repeatedly sexually abused for years. I had lived with addicts, cons, and thieves and was betrayed by my own grandmother. Like meteors in space, they each crashed into me at different points of my journey. They changed my trajectory in ways I will never understand. Who would I have become had they helped me along my way rather than obstructed it? And who would they have become had they not endured a lifetime of pain themselves? But I was a child and unable to course correct. These traumas were what I knew. They were all I had to prepare me as I dug into my freshman year of high school life in Union City, hormones raging, voice changing, and navigating the new world of girls.

I was falling deeper and deeper into the darkness, although my mask radiated a false light.

CHAPTER 7

After the skirmish with my uncle, my grandmother completely changed. She didn't look at me or treat me as you would expect a grandmother to treat her grandson. Instead, she looked at me with resentment and disrespect. I lived with her daily reminder that I was unworthy for another year before we finally moved out, but by then I was fifteen and the damage was done. My mother found a unit at Mission Sierra Apartments a few minutes away from my grandmother's in a neighborhood called Seven Hills. It was a two-bedroom apartment in a complex that was supposed to be modeled after a California mission. The entrance to the leasing office had an arched entryway and wrought iron bars in the shape of a cross over a square cut-out in the facade. But other than that, it was just a plain, regular apartment complex.

So, here we were, the four of us sharing a two-bedroom apartment. My brother and I shared a room, my sister had a room, and my mother once again sacrificed by making the living room her sleeping quarters. We had grown accustomed to living in spacious homes with front and back yards, with our own rooms and plenty of extra space. Now we were packed in like sardines, but for the first time in a long time we were at peace. We were free from the drama and chaos. We were free from the abuse and trauma. We were free from the constant taint of toxic air. This freedom made this tiny two-bedroom apartment feel like a thirty-five-bedroom mansion.

Once again, we were latchkey kids. I still reflect on how this particular circumstance changed my life forever. I was a child, but I shouldered the responsibility of an adult. As the oldest, I bore the unrelenting burden of responsibility for me and my sister's safety and well-being. Without a nurturing parent or adult to talk to about the ups and downs of our days, we felt a coldness, an indescribable absence that was always there. And we had a lingering anxiety that something could go wrong at any time. This stress, more than anything, was a deep dread at the bottom of my soul.

I didn't feel free and happy-go-lucky like my other friends. They had someone at home to talk to, lick their wounds, prepare snacks, and help with homework. We weren't hungry or in any immediate danger, but my spirit was thirsty for nurturing, and my heart was worn down from wearing adult shoes without ever having had the chance to wear my own. I had already learned how to compartmentalize—be one thing on the outside and another on the inside—because of my father. But being a latchkey kid forced me to even more deeply separate my worlds so that I could pass through life with somewhat of a semi-normal existence.

I was glad to get away from the chaos of my uncles and the glare of my grandmother, but by now I knew that a new location didn't always mean the end of trouble. In fact, I had come to expect trouble. No longer would I be hopeful only to be bitterly disappointed. No longer would I open my heart only to have it crushed to pieces. I had been a child when I was expected to be a man. For me, now, there was nowhere in the world that was safe. I was slow to trust and quick to retreat. I was always in fight-or-flight mode. What I didn't realize then is that everything I was feeling were the symptoms of post-traumatic stress disorder. Even when I first heard the term PTSD years later, I didn't put it together. Wasn't PTSD associated with people in the military coming back from war? Or people who had faced a life-threatening ordeal, or who had seen horrible things that they couldn't erase from their minds and their souls? Then I realized I had experienced all of that. I didn't have to go away to war, because the war was deeply rooted in my ancestral soil, and now it was now being waged within me. Soldiers often hide their trauma because they can't afford to look weak. We see this with police officers and other people whose jobs are to be protectors, but what about fathers and mothers, sons and daughters, who mask their pain, who push it down and hide it away, only to pass it along to the next generation? Was that not just as damaging? PTSD (Post Traumatic Stress Disorder)—four letters that spell a lifetime of suffering, even if you don't know you have it.

Like many other people who have PTSD, I tried to suppress my feelings and went on as if nothing was wrong. I was just beginning my high school journey. I didn't want to be that kid, the kid with the issues. Blending in was key. Sports allowed me to do that.

And Mike and Ron.

Mike Phipps was my first friend at Alvarado Middle School in Union City. I was new in the eighth grade as others were reuniting after summer vacation, exchanging their stories of what they had done during the break. I found myself alone. But before I knew it, a boy approached me and began talking to me as if we had known each other for years. He had a broad forehead, full cheeks, deep-set eyes, and a pointed chin. He told me his name was Mike. He was unassuming, affable, and most of all, funny. I was awkward, shy, and serious.

We quickly discovered that we lived two blocks from one another, which made it easy to cultivate our new friendship. The glue that bonded us almost immediately was our shared desire to belong to someone. Mike wasn't worried about trying to be popular or tough, and neither was I. We just both needed a friend. We became that for one another.

What brought us even closer was landing on the same Little League baseball team that year. I was a good player, but Mike was an outstanding all-star player. He was a natural with a fast bat and powerful speed. In so many ways, Mike was the antithesis of my father. His laugh and smile were infectious. He was always rooting for the underdog and thought everybody, whether friends or enemies, should find a way to coexist and enjoy life. He was slow to anger and didn't harbor resentments, but if threatened or cornered, he'd have no problem protecting himself. Even though we were the same age, he seemed to fill the void that was created by both my father's presence and absence. For the first time, with Mike, I felt like I could enjoy being a kid.

37

A typical day involved riding around on Mike's Diamondback dirt bike, our primary mode of transportation. We took turns pedaling while the other rode on the handlebars. We had everything we needed in our neighborhood to stay fully contained. Other than going to and from baseball practice, there was no need to venture out unless it was to meet up with friends to play sports, our hood against theirs.

In addition to sports, we played video games and talked to girls. We went to the mall and movies and whatever else we could do to occupy our minds. Mike's house was headquarters, and that's where we hung out the most, especially during summer breaks. We ate all his food and just played Intellivision all day, every day.

I loved sleeping in during the summer days, and there were plenty of days I'd wake to find Mike already in my room, anxious to get the day started, even though that meant hurrying up to do absolutely nothing. We were on a schedule: wake, hang out, ride, play, eat, sleep, repeat the next day. Mike was truly the closest person to me besides my family. From the day we met in eighth grade until my family moved across town in eleventh grade, we saw each other every single day. Only when he went to college at Jackson State University in Mississippi was there a daily break in seeing each other.

Ron Blackburn and I met later in the eighth grade, though we would not become close until our junior year in high school. He had a very different background than Mike's. Mike had two parents and a brother at home, a nice house with two cars, and plenty of food in the cupboards. Ron's mom was a divorced single mother—his father was virtually absent—and he was in an environment in which he mostly needed to fend for himself, much like my life. To the outside world, Ron was a tough guy who was always fighting. He did his share of dirt, and he kept up his bad-boy image for the streets. What he found in me was somebody who wasn't intimidated by him or afraid to fight him but also somebody who saw him for his gifts and talents, not his grit.

Ron ran the streets a lot and was connected to a clique that worked the streets. He and his crew had to do whatever they had to do to help provide for their families and hustling was just part of life, but they were guys that I liked and considered friends. They just lived in a different part of town, so I didn't judge their hustle and they respected my choices also.

Kids in my neighborhood got jobs at the local pizza parlor or movie theatre. Kids in Ron's hood hustled. I was the place he sought refuge from it. I was the person he confided in. I was the person who challenged and checked him. I was the person who forced him to see his potential and not his regrets. The three of us—Mike, Ron, and myself—became a crew throughout our high school years. We were all we needed as we each tried to navigate the challenges of surviving, of getting through high school and succeeding as young Black men. These were my guys, brothers, protectors and family. I loved them. They held my history and secrets and I held theirs. They made my life make sense. They gave me a tribe to belong to. After moving around my entire youth, they were the home base that provided me the security I needed and longed for.

PART 3

*"Herein lies the tragedy of the age:
not that men are poor—all men know
something of poverty; not that men are
wicked—who is good? Not that men are
ignorant—what is truth? Nay, but that
men know so little of men."*

—W.E.B. Du Bois,
The Souls of Black Folk

CHAPTER 8

My eighteenth year proved to be a turning point for me. After graduating from high school, I was prepared to start college life at Morehouse College in Atlanta, Georgia. I had been accepted to a summer program prior to the start of the fall classes. Though my father was still largely absent, he assured me that he had saved enough for my college tuition. I relied on that as I filled out my college applications. But when the time came for me to leave, there was no tuition and no follow-through behind his promises. While I watched my friends leave for college one by one, I found myself left behind, in need of a job.

I began working as an operator for a telephone company, and that's when I began to hear the whispers of self doubt and self loathing growing louder: *You're not good enough. You're not smart enough. You're not handsome enough. You don't have enough money.* These were voices and statements that I had heard all my life, only they had always come from someone else's mouth. Now they were in my head. My inner voice that had been dormant all these years was speaking. And it was proving to be more destructive than any external voice that had ever said a word to me.

In high school I lived in a bubble. I was a good athlete, so I always did well in sports. Since the age of seven, I played year-round sports, so I got plenty of attention for my playing from coaches and fans. I lived at home with mom, so there was family, food, clothing, and shelter. But after graduation, without the scaffolding and activity of high school, these internal voices of unrest crept in. I know they had always been there, but until now it had never been quiet enough to hear them. I had always been around family or friends or turmoil. I had a daily routine, which didn't require thinking or feeling, because I was simply following orders: go to school, go to practice, take your sister with you to play, clean your room, be home for dinner before the streetlights turn on, eat, wash, sleep. I lived inside the safety of this routine, which was regulated by my mom. When it came time to begin living my own life, everything around me grew so quiet that all I could hear was my own voice tearing me down.

Year after year, I stockpiled toxic emotions in a place that was designed for love. All the scar tissue overwhelmed my system to the point that I no longer had the capacity to feel the love that might have been underneath. Instead of feeling worthy, I felt less than. Instead of confidence, I had insecurity. Where the feeling of *I can do anything!* was supposed to reside, I had doubt and craved external approval. Where the feeling of safety was supposed to be, all I felt was abandonment. So, I did what anyone would do. I responded to the voice of doubt and fear and insecurity by trying to drown it out. This was the origin of the undesirable trait of imposter syndrome.

To avoid facing all these emotions, I began a nonstop race toward external success. Every day in high school, I was in constant pursuit of something. I had a desperate desire to be happy and was willing to do whatever it took to get it, no matter the cost. My childhood mask had protected me; my high school mask was designed to gain affection. But you can only put off facing emotions for so long. Like missing payments for a loan, the interest begins to build. I had become an expert at putting off my painful emotions, replacing them with superficial highs. I had learned that if I did something impressive, people gave me praise. That praise made me feel powerful. Getting praise made me feel good about myself, and feeling good about myself had covered up all the pain that was now coming to the surface. To stop this pain from overwhelming me, I had to try a new tactic—to run.

I wasn't running anywhere in particular. I was running *away*. I was running away from the opportunity to heal, because running was easier and less painful than addressing the truth. Striving toward nothing was still easier than thriving inside my truth. I sought praise, praise, praise. I needed it. I did whatever I had to do to earn it. External praise was my main goal, because it was the only thing holding me up. It didn't matter if I was enjoying myself or not. The praise was the outcome, and the outcome fueled my existence.

It was during this time that the adult women I worked with at the telephone company, some single and some married, began paying attention to me. Maybe it was my youth and innocence. Maybe it was my personality. Or maybe they sensed a vulnerable energy in me that told them I was open prey. The more they flirted, the more validated I felt and the less I heard my inner voice reminding me that I was worthless. These women, who were in their twenties, thirties, and forties, made me feel special. The less I heard the unrest, the more I flirted back. The more I flirted back, the bolder they became, until eventually the intoxication of it all drowned out the voices altogether.

At first, the flirting was just innocent fun, trying to pass the time on particularly slow workdays, but one day things escalated. A woman named Melody, who was at least ten years older than me, was more persistent than the others. Our flirtation broached the limits of regular banter. She was not shy about telling me how attracted she was to me and how badly she wanted things to get physical. She even invited me to her home. I would politely decline, but it never deterred her from asking again and again. As a red-blooded eighteen-year-old man, her words appealed to my ego, my drive, and my insecurities.

She didn't know my background or that I had issues with my father and family. All she knew was that she liked what she saw. She wanted me, and she was saying all the right things. Her words dripped like honey, and I began to respond to her praises. One day, over my better judgment and values, I reluctantly agreed to meet her at her home during lunch. This would be the first of many yesses that should have been nos. After some small talk, she became aggressive and things began to get physical. I was taken aback at first. There was this sense of obligation I felt to comply with her needs that overshadowed mine. I really didn't want to be there, and I wanted to leave, but the hold of

45

validation had me, and I couldn't break free. I saw how much she liked it, and I wanted her to. Her pleasure made me feel important, desired, and wanted, but I did not enjoy myself at all. For me, the act felt empty. She was married, and she had convinced me—or I had convinced myself—that it was okay to do what we did. But I felt used, dirty, sad and lost after this, the very same way I felt as a young boy after my babysitter had her way with me. What was supposed to be a triumph of ego turned into a moment in which I dug a deeper and wider hole into my already rather large pit of worthlessness. Just like that, yet another layer of disconnect was added to my heart, but this time it included a larger portion of my soul to boot.

After that encounter, I descended into a place I had never been before. I would stay in this place for the next twenty years or so, which got deeper and wider as the years ticked by. I saw women as objects of validation and sex as a transactional tool for redemption. It was never about physical pleasure. It was about trying to feel wanted, needed, and valued. I was trying to find the affection, praise, and confidence that alluded me all the years prior. I so needed it, by any means necessary, and was willing to pursue it.

That one act, that one decision, the inability to use my common sense and value system in that moment set me on a multi-decades-long destructive course. It's amazing how one bad choice can forever alter your life. I was a meteor colliding into women who in turn suffered pain and anguish because of my web of lust, deceit, lies, and manipulation. I told women I loved them when I didn't mean it. I took advantage of their desperate need for attention and affection to selfishly serve my own.

After sleeping with Melody and learning how much older women responded to me, this became my primary pursuit to boost my self-esteem and satisfy my craving for validation. I jumped in with both feet. Sleeping with a married woman changed me in a way that I hadn't expected. The day my dad walked off the football field had changed me, because though he was physically still in our lives, he had abandoned me. That one decision to sleep with Melody was me abandoning myself.

My spirit stood there, crestfallen, as I walked off on my chance to be a different, decent man.

From that point on, other older women hit on me with the same intensity that Melody had, and I can only assume that she had kissed and told. I entertained a few of them and very quickly became dependent on the attention they were giving me. I needed it, in fact, because it was the only thing making me feel like the man. And because I was still so focused on myself and not how my actions affected others, I started to develop a sense of entitlement. As far as women and their affections went, my sense of respect and chivalry was going out the door.

The more I slept around, the less I saw women as people. They more and more became mere objects of my dysfunctional behavior. I became blinded to their need to feel connection and relationship and instead saw only legs, breasts, faces, and ass. I didn't recognize that their own emotional wounds and deficits drove their behavior and motivation toward me. Ninety-nine percent of these women were using sex with me transactionally to fill their own emotional deficits. I didn't analyze or question the intent or meaning behind any of these physical relationships. Frankly, I was singularly focused on drowning out my pain and wasn't interested in looking at the truth.

Years later, my warped view and misunderstanding of what women needed would lead to two marriages, both of which I was emotionally incapable of committing to. I had been unfaithful to both women, broken my vows in both marriages. It wasn't because I was incapable of integrity, keeping my word, and being a committed, devoted husband. It was because my model of what a husband was supposed to be was based on my father and all the other broken men I saw married and perpetuating a negative cycle of chaos. In addition, I was groomed by the men in my life to embrace the notion that a man was supposed to have more than one woman. That as a man our honor and duty was to ourselves and under no circumstances were we to become "whipped" and controlled by one woman. Most important was the honor code of never being honest if we were caught. Deny, deny and deny was the motto and honesty was for the weak. This was my conditioning and I didn't have a shot at a successful relationship with this unenlightened advice and way of relating to a woman who gave me her heart to protect. I was doomed to fail because my heart was corrupt. What I thought was right and normal turned out to be wrong and dysfunctional. It was not until I became a father myself that I would be able to see what had been broken in me and begin to right these wrongs. It took new life to bring about old redemption.

I must stop here and speak briefly about my marriages, as these were both pivotal points in learning who I was and being able to heal once and for all. A major note is that like attracts like, and we tend to draw to us reflections of who we are. Both women are beautiful, intelligent, and can hold a great conversation. These were women who were and are awesome human beings. Their mistake was to trust and love me. Like me, they also had major daddy issues, which in essence created a dynamic of unhealthy codependency.

The first time around, I was twenty-three when we got engaged. I wasn't in love and knew it was not the right match, and although she knew it as well, I felt pressure to conform and not let anyone down, namely our parents. Although I called the wedding off twice, I relented to the pressure of validation to follow through. My parents were very insistent on my marrying her, and given my past, I didn't have the internal fortitude or courage to do the right thing for me. Like Monica, then Melody, and now Mom and Dad, I put the needs of others before my best self and made yet another wrong decision at what otherwise would have been a seminal moment of growth for me. Within weeks of being married, I was trying to get out. I did my best to coexist, but I wasn't successful. I eventually mustered up the courage to get a divorce, but not without paying a toll in my soul.

The second time I was in my early 30s and on the other side of most of my trauma. What I didn't know was lurking was toxic residue. The pressure this time was my religious convictions and social standing. I was single, successful, and unmarried and needed a wife. My mask drove me to completing the picture. I also was following the scripture "it's better to marry than burn." So what did I do? I placed myself in the middle of a relationship, rushed a marriage, and went further down the rabbit hole.

How does an impostor enter into an authentic relationship? For me at least, the answer is dysfunctionally. I was determined not to repeat the errors, missteps, and bad judgment of my past. I was determined to live out my vows. I was focused, happy, and settling into a new beginning. Then the unexpected happened. I found someone that made me feel like the lyrics in the singing group Guy's Let's Chill song: "All my love is for you, whatever you want I will do, you're the only one I want in my life, for you I'll make the sacrifice." So, that's what I did. I went all in for the first time ever.

Soon after the marriage began, early challenges devastated me because for the first time in my life I went all in and trusted someone only to find myself reeling from disappointments and letdowns. Rather than handle them constructively in a way to protect the marriage, I allowed mistrust to grow and the feelings of rejection to take over. Slowly, I fell into my destructive patterns. My leap of faith into the relationship became tiny steps away from it, to the point where I once again used divorce as a tool. This time was much harder, though, because we had two beautiful children and because it was the first time I was honest about my past, maskless, and ready once and for all to live a life of vulnerability, authenticity, and truth. Had I stayed, I would've perpetuated the cycle. My leaving sent me on a healing journey that I am forever grateful for.

CHAPTER 9

I had stopped being a victim by becoming a victimizer. This is what my paternal grandfather had done. This is what my father had done. And now it was what I was doing. My life story was written before I was even born. What would my life have been had I had the power to write it myself? How was I supposed to know the difference between the life I inherited and was living out and the new life I had been created to live? It was very difficult for me to identify and see the truth, because I was trapped in a vicious cycle, living a life inside a closed loop of ego, fear, survival, and denial.

I had been programmed with this pattern of thinking, and I had fully internalized it. These patterns had become so power-ful that my physical body just repeated the patterns without me having to think at all. In other words, my unconscious mind was in control, working and reworking the conditioned patterns and responses. Mediocrity and failure were inevitable; the fear and anxiety this inevitability brought me could be relieved by women and material things. If I was feeling down or unsuccess-ful, I would call a woman to be the object of praise or purchase something that people desired and admired. And this is where I kept it, even when I might truly achieve something valuable. As soon as something looked like it might turn into something big or I found myself on the precipice of achieving something phenomenal, I would convince myself that it was too good to be true, that I was mediocre, then I'd fall back into the pattern.

Since I believed failure was inevitable, instead of increas-ing my efforts, I would pull back and take my foot off the gas. Rather than wait for the disappointment that I was convinced would come when it all fell apart, I could maintain control and pull the plug on my own terms. I believed things were not going to work out, and it was just a matter of time. As fate would have it, I was always right. Things always fell apart. The more things didn't work out, the more I used women and superficial objects to give me a temporary feeling of success, no matter how fleeting the feeling.

I was able to trace some of the origin of this thinking to the disappointments and abuse from my father. His broken promises and not showing up to do the things he promised taught me to lower my expectations and not trust. If my own father couldn't be there for me in the ways I needed, nobody could. I developed a practice of protecting myself by not expecting good things to happen in order to avoid the pain of disappointment. What hurt beyond words as a young boy motivated me to develop a new system to avoid this type of negative emotion as a young man. I didn't realize I was living inside a self-fulfilling prophecy. There have been many instances of self-sabotage in my life, almost always involving the two things I used to drown my pain: women and the power I gained from external praise. This is what mostly defined my twenties.

Even though I spent more time with Mike before we graduated high school, Ron had a better understanding of how I thought and understood how I operated because his childhood was similar to mine. Ron was very intelligent and desperate for relevance. He wanted to make a name for himself, and he carried his swagger accordingly. Women loved him too, and he and I would compete for notches on our belts. We were both very young and immature to be in live-in relationships with our then girlfriends which was a matter of necessity and survival. There was no childhood home with fond memories to go back to, so we found ourselves both cohabitating with people we knew we could at least depend on, even if they weren't the loves of our lives. We were both living inside co-dependent dynamics which took a toll after a while, especially being in our early twenties, so we chatted and decided we'd be better off moving in as roommates than continuing to live with women because we felt we had no place else to go. We decided to get a place together and become roommates. This was a couple years after we graduated from high school. We were opposite ends of the same battery, simultaneously repelling and charging one another in our quest to feel complete.

Meanwhile, Mike was away at college. We were still brothers, despite the distance and our new lives. When he came home for a break during his sophomore year, all we wanted to do was catch up, hang out, and relive our summers during middle school. But he was sick with chickenpox and was quarantined at home, so instead we spoke to each other by phone every single day that summer. Our conversations mainly consisted of me asking him if he was still sick, urging him to recover as soon as he could, and then laugh and talk about nonsense as we did when we were younger.

I thought this would be the summer of recapturing our youth. Instead, I had to say goodbye to my first real friend. Mike died unexpectedly from an illness he had been battling all summer. He was twenty-one. I always knew chickenpox was more severe in adult men than with boys. Although it is rarely fatal, it proved too much for Mike's body to fight off. I'm not sure if he had other underlying health conditions or a compromised immune system, but he never recovered. I wasn't too caught up in figuring out exactly what went wrong. All I know is that my last visit to him in the hospital was surreal. He was unconscious and never woke up. I said goodbye to him with his eyes closed, not knowing if he heard me or not. He was wearing a Walkman with his favorite song on repeat, Pete Rock and CL Smooth's "Reminisce." To this day, anytime I hear that song, I become immediately emotional and nostalgic and think of my man Mike.

Even now, I'm incapable of finding the words to describe how devastated I was. I carried so much pain: my father's abusive words and abandonment, sexual molestation, my grandmother's hate. No one understood my suffering the way Mike did. No one listened to what I had to say or gave my words and feelings any worth the way Mike had. Mike was my brother, whose family life represented everything I always wished for. When he died, that perfect dream of a life that I had died with him, and again my life was changed. The trauma from this loss was almost more than I could bare. The only thing that kept me going was my newly restored relationship with my father which was feeding parts of me that laid barren all the years prior and my youthful exuberance that was determined to succeed in life in honor of Mike's memory. I thought his death shouldn't be in vain and I would make something of myself as a tribute to him. Yes, another major layer of disconnect found me, but I still had some light in my eyes that hoped for more, for better, for purpose.

Mike was buried the same day I attended first day at the University of San Francisco. I had enrolled to pursue my bachelor's degree, which I hoped to receive in 1996. This day was a paradox that no day has even come close to touching. On one hand, I had to bury my best friend, home for summer break from college, dead at twenty-one. On the other hand, I was starting a new chapter in college myself. These two things juxtaposed together represented the best potential and the worst realities of my life.

George Michael Phipps was friendly, likeable, funny, intelligent, and one of those rare good souls God lets us borrow for oh-so-short of a time. He had no enemies. It didn't take much to make him happy. He was easily embarrassed and hated to be teased. I think the most endearing memory of him was his love for dancing. He was a great dancer and loved to show off his moves anytime he heard a beat. He also knew how to breakdance. Mike had rhythm, and he knew how to make it look good. What I learned from him was that a man could be inherently decent, that anger didn't always have to be simmering beneath the surface, and that when nurtured, a young boy could grow to become a great man. If only he had the chance to reach his fullest potential.

I can't remember a day that went by after his death that Ron and I didn't talk about Mike. There were three of us, then we were two, and we frankly never really got over that. We were like a three-legged stool that now had to find a way to find balance, especially without Mike's grace and humility to temper our personalities, which we desperately needed.

Ron and I were at the start of our twenties, in a competition to see who could get the most girls. He had a big personality that could fill up the entire room. He had a big ego and wasn't humble in the least. He loved to roast people, and he prided himself on getting under peoples' skins with his wisecracks and insults. He wasn't malicious; he just enjoyed making people laugh at the expense and embarrassment of others. After all, this was how it was for us growing up. Even so, Ron was a fierce protector of his family and friends, and he was loyal to a fault. He would grow easily frustrated whenever I got praise. He was often seen as the troublemaker, but only because I kept my bad-boy antics under wraps, while he carried his out in the open. But even I knew it was time to start growing up. As lost as we both were, it was time to try to find our way.

CHAPTER 10

After feeling powerless all my life up to this point, I was on a quest to gain as much power as I could. I knew I didn't want to work at a telephone company forever, but I needed an exit strategy before I could fully quit. A couple years prior in 1989, my cousin, Lamont Penn, had built a name for himself as a rapper under the name of MC Sergio. He was a local celebrity in Oakland and the San Francisco Bay area in general, especially after the song for his hit single, "Oakland Strip," made it onto KMEL, the big local radio station in town. He needed a manager, so I enrolled in San Francisco State University's Recording Industry Program to learn the ropes of the music business. This isn't to be confused with the University of San Francisco which I also attended and earned a BS degree. I paid my tuition using the money I had saved working at the phone company. I hadn't even hit twenty yet, learning about a new industry, when I launched my first entrepreneurial endeavor, Juice Records, which was my first record company. In addition to my cousin, I took on a few more acts and introduced Ron to the industry. Ron and I were grinding.

I was still working a full-time job, studying at San Francisco State, and putting out records. I was starting to see real money. Juice Records was building a name for itself. My cousin was busy performing and putting out more songs, and my latest group—which featured three high school friends: Frankie J (Frank Gibson), Den Fenn (Dennis Thomas), and DJ Nuttz (Josh Gomez)—had its own hit song on the radio, "Big Mamas." Juice Records was earning good money.

One day at home, Ron and I were sitting on the couch in the condo we shared looking at *The Source* magazine. There was a photo shoot of Diddy, who at the time went by the name

Sean "Puffy" Combs. At that time, he was up-and-coming and nowhere near the level of success he would become known for, but something in that photo resonated with Ron, and he decided he wanted to be just like Diddy. From that moment, he became fixated on becoming a record executive. He didn't know much about the business, but he knew he wanted whatever he perceived Diddy having, so he made a choice that day to go after it no holds barred. I encouraged him to enroll into the same program I learned so much in, and he worked hard at it and studied.

While attending San Francisco State University, he landed an internship at Universal Music in San Francisco. His boss was a young Oakland native and music head by the name of Diallobe Johnson. As fate would have it, all these years later, Diallobe is one of my closest friends. Ron never looked back. He drew his passion from an earlier disappointment he didn't want to repeat. He would tell me all the time in private that he regretted not working harder at football in high school to earn a scholarship, and he wouldn't make that mistake twice by not taking the record business seriously.

His personality and ego were better suited for the music industry than mine. He liked the flash, swag, and fast pace. He fell in love and dove in.

I wound down Juice Records because I grew weary of the shady characters and egotistical acts, but Ron was ramping up his own career, working with other acts around the San Francisco Bay area. This also coincided with my moving out to buy my own condo. I was twenty-four by now. Even in the midst of working full-time and running Juice Records, I was also a full-time undergraduate student at the University of San Francisco. With Juice Records closed, I was able to devote all my time to my corporate career and finishing my BS. Although we lived apart, we were still best friends. We didn't hang out as often, but we talked on the phone a lot. He was chasing his come-up in the music business, and I found myself bit by the entrepreneurial bug again. This time it was real estate investing.

A couple years after buying my condo, I began investing in real estate. I converted my second bedroom into a home office, and in a couple short years, my cousin Lamont Penn and I had amassed a valuable real estate portfolio. I was young and single, making serious money and thriving. Life couldn't be better. In the midst of all this prosperity, Ron came knocking.

He had an idea of a record company he wanted to start, but the only problem was he enjoyed the creative side more and didn't have much interest for the dollars-and-cents aspect of the business. He had a dream of creating a company modeled after Diddy's Bad Boy Records and knew he couldn't do it alone. I wanted nothing to do with it. I was young, financially independent, and was building my own empire. He went to work selling me on his dream and wouldn't leave me alone until I agreed to help him. He was convinced he needed my help, and there was nothing I could do to convince him otherwise. He was also savvy enough to know he needed my financial resources to bankroll the startup, which was something I could easily do without flinching.

Things happened fast with Ron's creative vision and my business savvy. We named our company Ronlan Entertainment, and we began laying the foundation for its long-term success. Being in it with my best friend was motivation enough, and seeing him happy and full of purpose inspired me. Our star was rising fast.

I turned to one of my mentors for business advice on how to scale the record company, and I was encouraged to seek outside investment and to stop putting my own money at risk, to keep it working for me in real estate. Although I had from time to time used outside investors to acquire property, they weren't strangers and were high-net-worth individuals I knew personally. I didn't have a network of investors that were into putting money into record companies, so I had to venture outside my personal network to find dollars. After interviewing a number of interested investors, we partnered with a man named Steve Kelly. He was the CEO of a company called M&A West Inc. Steve had built a successful boutique venture capital company, and he had a number of exciting start-ups that he had helped build. Many were either getting acquired by a larger company or going public with IPOs. He was a brilliant investor, one of the reasons I wanted to be in business with him. So, not only did I find a willing investor, I found a new mentor who could teach me new skills.

Steve was a former Wall Street investment banker who, like many before him, wanted to get closer geographically to Silicon Valley. Like Jeff Bezos and others, Steve saw the Internet as the future and wanted to be in a position to cash in. After a quick negotiation, we sold him 25 percent of the company for one million dollars. We were nowhere near being profitable yet, though our music and artists were hitting the Billboard charts. By now, I was twenty-eight years old and really had no idea what I was doing, but I trusted my instincts and made the deal. I was nervous and a little intimidated, but that didn't stop me.

The real estate investment business was going strong, and we had been accumulating assets for long-term holds that generated lots of passive rental income. I was a long way from that poor kid living with a mom that worked three jobs and still could barely make ends meet. I never really thought twice about quitting my corporate job of eleven years, which had me on the fast track to the executive floor. I was more alive, and it was more natural for me to be my own boss. So, running the real estate company and holding down my responsibilities to Ron and my new record company felt natural. Even though real estate was lucrative and stable and produced enough income for me to be able to retire, the record company was where things were really heating up.

During one of our routine update meetings, Steve shared with us a vision he had to create a dot-com sister company to our record company. He told me he wanted to buy a shell company that was a bankrupt and defunct formerly publicly traded company that still had its public stock. Although the shares were worthless, they were active. We would place our new venture inside the shell, which would breathe new life into the dead enterprise. New life inside this old company would once again create value, and the shares would once again be worth something. This was a plan that would make us millions. I was really running now.

We came up with the name "volumne-city.com". We were going to make our catalog of music available online and get other record companies to license us their catalogs of music so we could put them online. The premise was, instead of buying music in stores, people could listen on their computers using the Internet. We built the new site, uploaded our catalog, and began testing. It all worked exactly as planned, and it was amazing. I had never seen anything like it before, and it felt like we were building a rocket to travel to Mars. This was 1999, two years before Napster.

Our model didn't allow downloads but instead sold subscriptions for people to access and enjoy music online anytime, as long as they had a computer and could connect to the Internet. There were no smartphones yet, and Scott's initial valuation on paper for volumne-city.com was ninety million. Each of us—Scott, Ron, and I—owned 33 and a third percent of the company, meaning our paper stock, pre-exit, was thirty million dollars. Oh, this was just too good to be true. And there it was. The old pattern. The old conditioning. The feeling of not being good enough for something like this. The feeling of being an imposter. Doubt hit me hard, and I began to spiral.

Everyday, those negative voices just got louder and louder. When they reached a fever pitch, I started to lower my expectations. "Don't get your hopes up," I heard myself say, just like when I was growing up and had to tell myself, "Dad isn't coming, so don't get your hopes up." Once that thought and feeling took hold, self-sabotage kicked into full gear. I began to convince myself, despite what was happening in reality, that this was never going to happen. It was too good to be true and this time next year I would not have thirty million or anything even close to it.

All that doubt and anxiety caused my focus and energy to drift. The bubble always burst, didn't it? I was just waiting for it to pop. Just a matter of time. I started delaying deliverables and not meeting deadlines. I started prioritizing other things. Steve kept pushing for results. I was waiting for it all to go bad.

Our record company was thriving and actually making national moves, and volumne-city.com was nearing readiness for market. Deep down, though, I was still waiting for everything to go bad. When things finally did take a turn toward bad, it was way beyond anything I could have imagined. In an instant, one of the greatest periods of my life went to the very worst.

CHAPTER 11

The night of April 20, 2000, Ron was shot and killed at a record release party. Of the three of us—Mike, Ron, and me—I was the only one left, and I felt truly alone. Ron was the positive, happy-go-lucky, fun side of our partnership and of my life. In the aftermath of his death, instead of honoring his legacy and finishing what we started, I quit. I was already in self-sabotage mode, and losing my best friend was more than justification to quit, as far as I was concerned. I've heard the saying "live a life with no regrets," but that was never my song. I made regrets. I quit on Ron's legacy, I quit on Steve, and I quit on me. I didn't have the courage or confidence to finish what we started, and nothing or nobody could pull me out of the deep pit I found myself in. I fell into a deep depression and no longer had a will to succeed at anything. I stopped working and lived off rent from my real estate business, and I let the record company and volumne-city.com die slow, excruciating deaths.

I had employees, recording artists, and an investor to answer to, but all I could see was my pain. All I could see was my own suffering and my endless cycle of burst bubbles. I was selfish, I was oblivious, and I was unskilled at being vulnerable. Looking back on all of this now, I can see no real reason why anything had to be shut down. I could have asked for help, but I didn't. I decided there was no way to navigate all of the personal turmoil. I was young, but I had all the material resources I needed to finish what we started. I just didn't have the emotional strength or courage to interrupt my pattern of self-sabotage. Nor did I totally understand the self-destructive nature of imposter syndrome.

Of all the tragedy and trauma I've been through in life, losing Ron sent me into the greatest tailspin. I lost the only identity I had, although it wasn't real, my hope, my inspiration. I became cold-hearted, cynical, and self-serving. I became the pain I had stored up over all the years. All of the suppressed emotions came to the surface and took over, and the mask that held them at bay could no longer protect me or those around me from the wrath of my past. My sister told me her observation recently. She said, "When Ron died, you died with him. Whoever Landis was, was no longer. I lost my brother and there was no longer any light in your eyes." She was right. This was the final layer of disconnect that would not only shut me off from the rest of the world, the door was sealed to letting anything or anyone inside. I ceased feeling, living and thriving.

When my father died two years after Ron, there was nothing left in me to grieve, to bear witness to pain, to acknowledge the present. I resigned myself to a future of fears and worries brought about by a lifetime of disappointment and sorrow. This was my untreated and unacknowledged PTSD. I was certain life was out to get me. I was certain that anything good would be met with something far worse. I was certain that life, no matter how good it could get, would always have the last laugh.

What I had yet to learn was that in the face of trauma and infinite, consuming darkness, there is one thing that is even more powerful: love. I did not know it yet because any brief encounters I'd had up to now in my life were buried under years of scars, inaccessible to me. Even my mother's expressions of love were tempered by the walls I'd built up to protect myself. To my mind, Mike's and Ron's untimely deaths were my punishment for loving them. The act of "making love" with women was never really love. My "love" for my father was mired in desperation. I was incapable of coping with my traumas because I didn't have any notion of what unconditional love was.

Until I became a father.

PART 4

"Success is to be measured not so much by the position that one has reached in life as by the obstacles which he has overcome while trying to succeed."

– Booker T. Washington

CHAPTER 12

After Ron's death, I fell by default back into real estate full-time. I grieved and was depressed, and I lived off the passive income we accumulated through Penn & Graden Properties. I was emotionless, directionless, without any close interpersonal relationships to tap into. I just allowed time to wash over me, and I made no attempt to live a life outside of the dark space in which I was imprisoned. I remained in this state for quite a while, until I was nudged out of the darkness by the same entrepreneurial bug that had brought me this far. A new vision of building a different type of company emerged, and that spark gave me energy to get off the canvass.. When I was ready, I started a new real estate business, which I still own and operate to this day.

In 2001, I met a young lady named Nicole, who immediately piqued my curiosity and interest. I was getting a haircut, and she was getting her hair styled. We were at Oakland Dempsey's Designs, a salon owned by a husband and wife. I mentioned to Bryant, the husband of the co-owned salon—and my barber—that I was interested in meeting her. So, he and his wife introduced us. At the time, we were both in relationships, so we met but kept it moving. We stayed in touch for years, and later when we were both single, we began spending more time together. We knew we liked each other, and we both felt a love connection early on.

I was taken by her natural beauty and intelligence. She had emotional smarts, book smarts, and common sense. She wasn't materialistic; she was cerebral and laid back. Given my past with women, she was a complete departure from flirtations I had entertained before. We began dating. We spent a lot of time together, enjoying each other's company and hanging out.

After about a year, I proposed. I figured there was no need to keep playing around. I found the woman I knew I could build a life with. Why not get started? We married six months later, and a couple years into our marriage, our daughter, Riley, was born.

I panicked. While many new fathers experience pure joy, I felt fear. I was afraid I wasn't going to love her the way a parent is supposed to love a child. I didn't know how to do this. I sat next to Nicole a few days before Riley was born, placed my hand on Nicole's stomach, and felt the baby kicking. I thought all at once about her entire life and whether I would be able to provide her with the kind of paternal love I was never given. I worried every day during Nicole's entire pregnancy, which many might do, but I couldn't help thinking about my own father, wondering if I was even capable of fatherly love.

When the day finally came, I realized I had nothing to worry about. I fell head over heels in love with her from the first moment I saw her. No, I didn't have a father to emulate, but I had a mother who, despite having to work tirelessly to support us, still managed to nurture me and instill strong values in me and my siblings. Up until this point, I hadn't really been able to tap into them, but my potential for love had always been there, hungry and waiting to surface.

The day we took Riley home from the hospital, I was nervous about getting her and her mother home safely. They were such precious cargo to me. I had my brother and brother-in-law triple check that I installed the car seat correctly. They both just kept repeating, "Everything will be fine, and you're going to be a great dad." They had no idea at that moment how much I needed their confidence in me that day. Being a new father was a forever, life-altering moment, and I understood then that there is no more important role for me in my life. When my son, Caleb, came a couple years later, I was excited to have a son, and I wanted to make sure as a Black boy that he had a strong Black male role model. Every day, from the moment he was born, I have worked to live up to that responsibility, and believe that I have.

After twelve years, I made the very difficult decision to leave the marriage. With the children shuttling back and forth between us each week, it gave me insight into how difficult it must have been for my father to not be around to help raise us. I vowed never to abandon my children, and I continue to be very present, hands on and active in their daily lives. I provide a safe space for them to land in times of need or crisis, something I never had. I spend a lot of time talking, grooming, and nurturing my kids. I'm constantly trying to learn who they are, and I look for clues and glimpses of their gifts and talents. I analyze how they think. I take notice of the things they like. I pay attention to what inspires them and what scares them. Doing these things and always trying for more allows me to nurture them in ways that build them up. I'm especially focused on paying attention. I missed out on all that which I believe triggered my longing to run, to rely on external praise and accomplishment in order to fill the love-shaped hole in my soul.

When I was young, I thought that running was just me being driven to succeed. Even though I was labeled a leader early in life and known by others as a go-getter, I didn't understand enough about myself to really harness those attributes in a meaningful, positive way. I was always intelligent with lots of potential to accomplish great things, but I wasn't rooted in a real identity. I was living according to the way my past experiences had programmed me, regardless of what was actually happening around me. My greatest identity now isn't CEO. It's *Dad*. Only by becoming a father have I been able to look at my own father with a different perspective. In truth, I had never given up on him. He showed up here and there, and we did our best to form a relationship in later years, but I never truly understood him or why he did the things he did until I became a father. Opening up to tenderness and vulnerability with my own children helped me tap into the empathy and forgiveness I needed to ease my lifetime of anger and ache.

When my father came to my high school graduation, it was a big deal for me, because I had no expectations of him showing up at all. He even came to the family get-together afterwards.

Prior to that, I hadn't seen him much, and his presence in my life was always sporadic and inconsistent. But at my graduation, just the fact that he showed up at all made me feel like he loved me. When I was twenty-one, I read the *Autobiography of Malcolm X,* which changed my entire self-image. It was the first time in my life I felt proud in my own skin and empowered to pursue my goals despite not having a father around. I began to be very deliberate about what and who I wanted in my life. I made a conscious decision to forgive him and start over with a clean slate. I reversed our roles, and I reached out to him. I began to call him regularly and visit him as much as I could. He had moved back to San Diego. Over the next five years, we forged a kind of relationship. He helped me get my first real credit card, introduced me to golf, gave me advice and counsel, and just became a genuine close friend. He even opened up about his mistakes and regrets being a father and a husband. After he died, I came across all the Father's Day cards my siblings and I sent him during the years he was missing in our lives. He had saved all of them, even though we would send them off not knowing if he saw them or if he even cared.

I wondered how he must have felt not knowing his children as they were growing up. When my children were born, I realized how much pain he must have been in to witness our births, to feel the pure and rapturous love looking into our eyes for the first time and being incapable of living up to our needs. I always wondered why he didn't love us, but in the end I realized his greatest torture was that he didn't love himself. It was the pattern he could not break. But I did. And because I did, I know my children will have a chance to pass on a new pattern—one of love, empathy, kindness, and patience—to my grandchildren one day.

CHAPTER 13

Healing lifelong emotional injuries and discovering who you are once those old injuries are no longer defining you is a complicated and painful journey. Many victims of abuse blame themselves, as I did, but the picture is so much larger. When we are in the moment, it is impossible to understand that we are being yelled at, or hit, or abandoned because someone else, years before we were even born, did this to someone, who had done it to someone else, who had done it to the person abusing us. In that moment, all we can think is, *What did I do?* Instead, the question should be, *How can I break this pattern?* But even that is complicated, because we must learn the difference between temporary fixes and meaningful, lasting change.

When we are smack dab in the middle of our crisis, trauma, abuse, or neglect, all we can see is our immediate environment. Whether we fight back or take the blows, the offense is real and we are the victim, and the world doesn't understand our pain. Seeing beyond the immediate is nearly impossible during the moment, and afterwards we want to forget it. So the cycle remains, and as the victim we internalize our pain. The pain becomes part of us to the point where we accept it as part of our existence.

Whether it was the car I drove or the clothes I wore, it was all for show. No matter how much money and assets I accumulated, I did so to keep score. There was a certain appeal I wanted to have to the outside world, because as long as people were looking at the outside, they wouldn't pay too much attention to the inside. I could cover up and distract from the ugliness and emptiness I felt on the inside with the purchase of beautiful things to wear on the outside. Even my promotions at work, which should've been purpose- and goal-driven, served to boost my self-esteem. The pursuit of upward mobility in my then chosen profession should've been leading me toward a higher calling, but instead it called to my need to validate the inadequacies I personified.

I was constantly seeking approval and affirmation from others through the things I achieved. If people weren't singing my praises, I worried that I no longer mattered. The boisterous accolades I heard from others was the only thing keeping simmering unrest, those old, internalized voices, at bay. When people weren't saluting me, my fears took hold. Fear of irrelevance, of being unworthy, created unhealthy needs that were only satisfied by external praise or buying material things. Marketers taught me to value material possessions, beauty, and the look of success. Photoshopped magazine covers removed acne, stretch marks, and blemishes, so I'd embrace an image of perfection even though the models brought those natural imperfections with them to the photo shoot. If it's natural, it's not an imperfection. It's beautiful.

They tell us to buy a certain body spray to get girls. They tell us to drive a certain car to be cool. They tell us to wear certain clothes to be sexy. They tell us, they tell us, they tell us. The proverbial "they" is nothing but people selling us goods and services for profit, only for them to get our money and live inside their very own imperfect lives just like we do. I could buy things to get an instant fix. So, in addition to driving myself toward nonstop accomplishments, I also amassed objects that people admired and desired, feeling a hit off that too. I got so good at it that, eventually, there appeared to be no difference between me and the version of me I presented to the world. I thought this was who I was.

I've often wondered when it started, some perfect storm of hiding to protect myself as a child, and when the adults around me became interested in telling me how they thought I should be instead of paying attention to who I was meant to be. One of the most frequently asked questions I got as a child was, "Who do you want to be when you grow up?" It was always a trick question. They weren't really interested in my answer. They were waiting to hear the "right" answer, which was: doctor, lawyer, policeman, or fireman.

At five, what did I know about those professions or any profession? Nothing. How could I forecast and comprehend a profession before I could even comprehend being a kid? Unfortunately, I did get the point. And if I wanted to be safe and be in the good graces of those around me, I knew I had to aspire to things and ways of being that people praised instead of finding the true calling and purpose planted deep in my soul. Our society relies on everyone conforming, on everyone being the same. Homogenous. Status quo. Don't make waves. Fail at being homogenous, fail at life. That was the message I received.

What I wish is that they had asked what made me happy. What made me sad. What excited me. What frustrated me. With children, what's essential are values and emotions, ideas and play and learning, not jobs or future success. Was I a visual, kinetic, audible, or an oral learner? What type of activities did I naturally gravitate toward? My elders should have been discovering and uncovering me with me. Finding the traces of my gifts, passions, and talents and helping to cultivate them. Instead, all went unnoticed in the midst of so much turmoil, replaced with some false goal of happiness.

From then on, I believed becoming a doctor or lawyer was superior to anything that I hadn't yet aspired to become. It almost didn't matter anymore who I would eventually want to be when I grew up. If it was anything other than a doctor or lawyer, I would be deemed a failure by society's standards. Those became the standard by which I measured success and thus my self-worth. The power of my early conditioning was potent.

Although I know this early conditioning was false and have since found my purpose, even now if I'm in a room and someone asks if there's a lawyer or a doctor in the house, I notice how other people in the room still tend to elevate them to idol status. Even in a room full of professionals with the likes of engineers, real estate developers, or educators, the doctors and lawyers are still held to higher esteem. It was a great epiphany for me to realize how much social conditioning played a role in my effort to suppress the person I believed myself to be and the man I am today. A loving father. A social entrepreneur. A man capable of generosity, empathy, and relationships. The legacy of my father's dysfunction played a significant part, but I later came to understand just how much people outside the home influenced me too. Their ideals fit right in with the trauma, the PTSD, the abuse, and unworthiness, external expectations of things I would never become unconsciously planted in my young mind by all the adults around me telling me what I needed to be when I grew up.

No matter who we are, where we came from, or what we've been through, we all put on a mask at some point to hide our fears and insecurities. For me it has been both a shield and a magnet. A shield protecting from real and perceived dangers in my childhood, that prevented me from maturing. A magnet pulling me toward unhealthy attention to fill the void in my heart and ego.

Money, muscles, cars, clothes, charm, and girls, I've had it all, trying to dress up my outside to hide the brokenness inside. I wanted the world to be proud of me, because I wasn't proud of myself. I wanted women to admire me, because I didn't know how to value my own heart.

Gucci, Prada, YSL, Chanel, Louis Vuitton, and Versace are made from the same leather, cotton, polyester, and wool as the merchandise sold in Target, Wal-Mart, JCPenney and Kohl's. But there was something about the logo of exclusive, expensive merchandise that made me feel exclusive and expensive. If I was able to feel exclusive and expensive, then at least for a few fleeting moments, I could feel unbroken.

I couldn't bear to be alone with myself. I stayed in constant motion, so I didn't ever stop to look in the mirror and see the real me. It was just easier and less painful to pretend, so I just got really good at acting.

CHAPTER 14

Most of us aren't even aware of our negative patterns. But if we can come into the knowledge that we are living out a pattern that isn't ours, and if we can discover the origin of it, we can become empowered enough to change it. Change, however, is complicated and many times painful. It's a dark, scary road to the light. We can get so used to living in the dark that the potency of the light can blind us. I say put on goggles and keep walking forward. It can also be rather lonely on that road, as many people are too comfortable being wrapped with the blanket of status quo, choosing the security of familiarity over the risk of freedom.

I know many people who think that because they were born into a bad situation, that is their natural destiny. They have adopted a limited belief about themselves because they only know the one life they were given. Regardless of whether or not they've felt sorry for themselves or have just resigned themselves to live below their calling, they didn't create the circumstances into which they were born. If someone believes their plight in life is to live in the margins, how do we convince them otherwise? If they believe being born on one side of the tracks or the other locks them into a predetermined future, how do we dispute that?

Starbucks founder Howard Schultz, Oracle founder Larry Ellison, and Oprah Winfrey, the first Black woman billionaire, all have something in common. They were all born on the poor side of the tracks. My point is, the only way to achieve, overcome, and accomplish is to truly believe you have the will and are capable.

I believe we are all born as pure organic, fertile soil. The soil has everything in it to receive, nurture, and grow whatever seed is planted. There is no special watermelon soil that's different from corn soil or that differs from lettuce soil. It's the seeds that carry the diverse DNA, and the seeds ultimately produce the fruit. If bad seed is planted in us, we produce bad fruit; if good seed is planted in us, we produce good fruit. My main point here is that we often forget we are the soil and identify with the fruit. Reflecting on my own journey, I see how my father's seeds grew alongside other bad seeds planted in me. Good thing I also had my mother's seed, which produced healthy fruit. As I got older, one of the most important lessons I learned was that I was the farmer not the harvester, that I had the power to sow and plant what I wanted, which would produce the fruit I wanted to bear.

Taking control of my mental, emotional, and spiritual diet put me on a course to cultivate my future. I realized that in order to live my truth, I had to set aside everyone else's. As a man of faith, I had a foundation in a greater truth that superseded my personal truth, but leaving me with enough leeway to drive where I wanted to go, to a place of my ultimate calling. It didn't mean that I always got it right out of the gate, but it didn't deter me from trying over and over until I got it right for me.

In my chosen profession of real estate development, there are a lot of complex sciences that come into play when building buildings. We study traffic patterns, air quality, available utilities, surrounding neighborhood conditions, and many other things, but the most important of all the things we study before building something is the soil. If the soil is polluted, we cannot build. If the soil isn't stable, we cannot build. If the soil has other issues or challenges, we cannot build. So what do we do? We fix the problems in the soil before we build. If we do not take the time to properly mitigate any detrimental issues we find with the soil, if we ignore them and build anyway, people can get sick in the case of contamination, and even die in the case of an earthquake.

Do some people circumvent what's right and build on problem soil anyway? Yes. At first glance, can you tell by looking at the completed building that it is built on top of a ticking time bomb? Not at all. Brand new materials, fresh paint, and no wear-and-tear looks impressive, but we know it's just a matter of time before something goes wrong, and we can only hope it isn't the worst-case scenario. So, just like people who grow up with bad seeds planted in our good soil, we become ticking time bombs. As the challenges of life mount, even when good seed is planted, something bad may have leached into our soil that poses risk to the fruit. Toxic people leave toxic residue. Sometimes it's microscopic and undetectable by the naked eye. It's easy to spot and correct bad fruit created by bad seeds, but how do we know if our soil has issues?

In the case of real estate, we can test for bad soil, and to remedy the problem, we will go as far as tearing down a building, removing the contaminated soil, importing clean soil, and rebuilding a brand-new building. If we go through that much time and expense for a piece of property that can be easily replaced, why wouldn't we do this for people? Are we not more important than a replaceable building? How do we then test our soil to free it of any issues so we can produce good fruit? What is that process and path? Touré Roberts calls this moving into "wholeness." Deepak Chopra calls this moving into "enlightenment." Richard Rohr calls this finding our "true self." I call it taking off the mask.

Our mask keeps us from living an authentic purpose-driven life. It's where we pull our mental, spiritual, emotional, and physical selves into total alignment with who we were created to be. If one makes that choice to pursue destiny, the road is wrought with pain and sorrow that ultimately leads to happiness and joy. It isn't easy to look in the mirror, acknowledge what you see isn't real, and then decide to learn what is true and what is false. It will require walking away from certain relationships or changing habits and hobbies. It is truly a purge of all things that contribute to moving us further away from who we are supposed to be and learning to embrace those things and people that bring us closer.

CHAPTER 15

On November 4, 2008, Barack Hussein Obama was elected the first Black president of the United States of America. Grant Park in Chicago was packed, and there was pure jubilation in the air. People were crying and hugging and celebrating. I saw Oprah overwhelmed with joy, shedding tears in wonder over what just happened. Not too far away, Jesse Jackson was doing the same thing. Watching President Obama and his family walk onto the stage was electric and awe-inspiring. As the four of them walked hand in hand so that we could celebrate with them, I felt chills all over my body. All I kept thinking was how proud I was to be an American and that I'd never forget this night the rest of my life. As Obama gave his speech, I hung onto every word, every syllable, and every pause. He reminded us that anything is possible and that "Yes, we can." I had goosebumps. I felt ten feet tall.

Eventually he finished his speech, gave everyone high fives and waves, and they walked off the stage. Just like that, America was changed forever, and I had been a witness. I didn't want the celebration to end and felt a little down after he and his family were out of sight. I wanted the moment to last longer. I wasn't done basking in his victory. I was full of hope, promise, and gratitude for all that I had experienced, which included voting for him.

Then a thought instantly occurred to me, and my joy turned to disappointment. Why was I at home watching this on television, when I should have been at Grant Park along with all the other people out there? Why didn't I have the courage and vision to travel to Chicago to live the making of history firsthand? These questions became a defining moment for me, because the emotions of this momentous occasion stirred something in me. I saw in Obama my struggle, but yet he triumphed where I failed. I knew his father was absent and that didn't hold him back from greatness. What about his journey and fortitude allowed him a path to achieve such great things where mine did not? I needed to know what was different between him and me, because I wanted what he had, the ability to reach my destiny as he had now reached his.

That's when a flicker of light went off in my brain. The thought hadn't occurred to me because I was so accustomed to living inside my small world that I forgot that there was an entire universe of experiences out there to see and explore: as a doer, not a consumer. That living in my mask kept me with tunnel vision that was fueled by keeping myself secure in my tiny world rather than taking risks in the broader universe. From that moment on, I vowed I would be a witness to and participant in significant events, local, national, and worldwide, in person as often as I could. I would no longer be a consumer of world events. I would be a contributor, which for me meant I needed to figure out what mattered to me. I needed to understand my values and motivations behind my goals. I needed to figure out my purpose and release the identity I lived within that gave me security and protection.

That's when I first began to take a hard look at myself and my life. I already knew how to persevere and overcome adversity. I already understood my talents and gifts and how to apply them. I already had an understanding of how I was wired and what my motivations were. I had been chasing my dreams for years. I had been self-employed for ten years with my real estate company the night Obama was elected, so I knew how to take risks and be successful. I made lots of money and lost lots of money, so I knew how to produce. I finished my MBA, so I knew how to focus. But something was still missing. I was living what I thought was an amazing life. I had accomplished on paper and in reality what other people praised as success. I had all the trappings and attributes of a well-put-together man and family man. I had the identity and persona of somebody to admire. But none of it was real. I was following a script, and I gave an Academy-Award-winning performance. I was living inside my false self, and now I was intent on learning my true self. If Obama could do it, so could I.

CHAPTER 16

President Obama's election opened a sleepy eye, and ironi-
cally, my first visit to the Obama White House jarred me
awake. Being in the room that day with all those brilliant people
overwhelmed my senses. I'd been on a journey. I'd done my
best to recognize the patterns of my father and interrupt them.
I worked hard to be the man that I thought at the time was an
emotionally and spiritually healthy man that was able to make a
name for himself. I honestly thought that I had been living the
ideal life. But that day in the White House, minding my own
business on a day in which I was positioning myself for even
more success it all came apart, the entire facade. Even though
I had spent plenty of time in therapy and worked hard at overcoming trauma and obstacles, I had more miles to run.

Up until then, I had followed the prescribed formula for
success. I didn't know that there is no formula for truth, and
that day, feeling like an imposter, the truth I lived within was no
longer good enough. I immediately became aware that all the
work I had done up to this moment was for my mind, but it was
my heart that needed to understand that lifelong traumatic conditioning would require me to venture into territory I didn't even
know existed—the dark, closed recesses of my heart and emotions that were buried so deep I didn't even know were there.
The years and years of suppressed emotions and the constant
churn of keeping it moving created a false sense of security.
The masks worked so well that they not only fooled the public,
they fooled me. Now, even though all my accomplishments
were real and I had put in the hard work with the accompanying
pain and sacrifice, I felt unworthy. I was a legitimate VIP guest
that surely belonged and fit amongst these distinguished guests,
but my deeply wounded emotional self wouldn't give myself

permission to see the value of who I was and what I brought to the table. I just felt the unworthiness of that nine-year-old boy.

I looked around at all the well-dressed and confident men and women. They all had a certain air about them. They were radiating confidence and accomplishment. I felt overtaken by my insecurities because they all truly exuded and believed for themselves what I had only been successful in achieving and cultivating externally: that I was important and successful. I just didn't believe it. Still, after all this time, I didn't believe it. I was sure it would only be a matter of minutes before they all realized I was a fraud.

After about an hour passed, I started to take note that all these people weren't smarter than me. Their accomplishments were just as impressive as mine. Then it clicked. I wouldn't have been invited to this meeting if I didn't belong in the room. Everything I felt was old. Older than me. Older than my history. I began to see just how impaired my image of myself and the world around me was due to years of pretending I was some-body else.

That's the first time in my adult life that I knew I was bat-tling a hidden problem that impaled me. Even though I was now a father, even though I had forgiven my own father before he passed, and even though, for all intents and purposes, I was liv-ing a successful life, I still needed help. There is no easy way to undo a life of tragedy and abuse. You must constantly watch for your own signs of distress and understand the triggers that set off past traumas. I knew that this challenge wouldn't go away if I ignored it, and if it went unexplored , my life would never reach the levels I was created to reach. So, what started as panic became panacea. Where I was gripped by fear and challenge, I quickly saw as opportunity. Here I was in the White House by exclusive invitation and felt I still wasn't good enough. The irony was that I was.

I began a journey of evolution. A journey of deep discovery. A journey of realization and a journey of final healing, restora-tion, and the last mile of wholeness. All the interpersonal and spiritual work I had done up to this point had brought me this far and served as a tremendous foundation for me to have a good life. If I wanted a life free from that toxic residue that was residing in those secret dark hidden places beyond feeling and expert eyes, I needed to be ready to handle anything I learned about myself. I was moving into no-man's land inside my heart that only I could reach if I so dared to go there. I could've kept the status quo, as life was good, but I decided it wasn't good enough, authentic enough, whole enough, or true enough. The afternoon I returned home from DC, I made a commitment to rid myself of the infection that was deep inside my heart that fueled this imposter thinking that kept me from living and see-ing a life of destiny and purpose. I knew I wasn't the only one that suffered in this way, so I also wanted to do it for them too.

I had to set my mental focus right, because I knew there was no magic pill. In an instant-gratification culture that likes quick fixes, this one had no timeframe for success, and there was no instant fix on the horizon. There was no expediting the healing process; it was going to be whatever it was going to be, and I needed to be prepared to see it all the way through no matter what ugliness came to the surface. I knew I preferred to live with my destiny than without it.

CHAPTER 17

So where did I begin? Even though I knew this was a heart issue, I had to make sure my mind was set up for success before I did anything else. If my mind couldn't handle the truth, then I'd never find it. The human mind is complex and mysterious, and there is much more that man doesn't know about the brain. Our repeated emotions become embedded in our bodies over time. This is why we can repeat habits without being consciously aware. If I'm driving home and lose myself in thought, I'm not thinking about the route or the dangers along the way. Soon, I'll end up in my driveway without remembering the dangers, risks, and route. Our habits drive our conditioned responses to everything we do. If I've always felt unworthy, then even when my accomplishments have opened the door for more opportunities, I'll still question their validity because I still believe I'm not worthy even though my work product has already demonstrated my worthiness. Feeling like an imposter wasn't created overnight, and freeing myself of that feeling also wouldn't happen overnight. I had to embrace that healing was going to be a process, although I much would have preferred it being a transaction.

The second most important takeaway is that the process never really ends. It's called a road to recovery, not the destination to recovery. It's a lifelong journey that needs to be consistently managed to stay in front of the forces that always fight to pull us backwards. Why? Because people aren't perfect, and we will deal with people everyday in our lives that have junk. Even if we are good, we may come across somebody who is not, and we need to protect our heart and peace. There is never a point where we go through so many hours of therapy, read a certain number of books, issue the necessary number of apologies and then are automatically healed. Healing is a verb, not a noun. It is a continuous action, not a state of being. When we get to the point when we can honestly say we've healed old wounds, then we shift from offense to defense. We were on offense as we pursued resolution, and we then must shift to defense to protect ourselves on the other side of clarity and wholeness. So, our job is never really done.

The never-ending nature of reaching and maintaining wholeness may sound discouraging to some, but really it is an opportunity to shift our perspective. Old wounds will be with me for the rest of my life even if healed, and under the right circumstances we are vulnerable to having old wounds pricked from time to time. Either we will maintain control over keeping them in check and under control, or we allow an opportunity for them to reopen and fester, which could create a window for them to gain enough power to cause trouble. So, my philosophy is to never get to the point where we believe we aren't vulnerable in being caught off-guard and unaware. I believe this is why Alcoholics Anonymous says once an alcoholic, always an alcoholic, even if a person hasn't had a drink in forty years. Emotional wounds should be treated similarly. We should always be protecting our hearts, lest we fall victim, unaware of forces that mean us harm beyond our control. The potential for trouble is always lurking, so it's better to be in control than to lose control.

A big part of maintaining a healthy emotional state is how we manage and regulate ourselves daily. For me, the journey to living inside my purpose with authenticity and truth is about shedding the limiting belief that I wasn't good enough. I had developed the fear that I didn't deserve success and that sooner or later everything would find a way to fall apart. This also applied to my love relationships. I believed I wasn't worthy of love and that after some time I would be abandoned. As a result, I didn't allow myself to trust nor fully invest all of me into anything or anyone. I guarded against the pain of being disappointed by not expecting too much or keeping my options open.

This was no way to live, for it limited my ability to reach my full potential in life, because I always held back. Allowing myself to fully embrace vulnerability, taking off the training wheels of trust, and allowing myself to believe that my value was based on God's calling and not by other people's opinions was part of the core work I needed to reinstall in my emotional operating system. Taking off the fears of failure and limitations and replacing them with positive reinforcement that I was more than enough and that my story was just as noteworthy as any other person's. I rid myself of the imposter syndrome and harvested my purpose by following a new way of thinking and feeling that led to new patterns and habits that needed to be practiced daily.

This is a never-ending battle between the forces of good and evil that have been going on since the dawn of man. If I depart from my tools and practices, I regress. If I stay focused, I move forward. Alcoholics Anonymous does a great job of helping its members recognize that the keys to success are to be sure never to "rest on your laurels," which means staying vigilant to remain sober and win the war one day at a time.

I have embraced the joy of being whole as a daily celebration. I wake up in the morning focused on victory and go to sleep at night taking account of my personal wins and losses and what I'm grateful for, each passing day striving to improve on the day before. I do this on days when things couldn't be more perfect and on days I'd rather forget. It isn't about the quality of day, it's about the health of my mind and heart. If my mind and heart are healthy and whole, the challenges of the day will always be kept in proper perspective. Just because we are doing the work and having balance and alignment doesn't exempt us from the contrary winds of life. When I have those times when I'm knocked on the canvas and despair starts to knock at my door, my day-to-day mentality always reminds me that the only way today's despair gets into tomorrow is if I invite it. Since I govern my thoughts as I've learned to do, I never invite despair to stay. I notice it, I acknowledge if it's trying to come inside, and I refuse it.

I want to pause here and talk a moment about the twenty-four-hour news cycle and how our culture aggressively reinforces emoji emotions. I believe we are living in an era where the true depth of human emotion is being minimized and numbed. I attribute this mainly to social media. Someone loses a loved one, we send an emoji and a few words. Someone is struggling, we send an emoji and a few words. My point in saying all of this is that the social engineering of society moves us further away from inflection and introspection. We are pushed deeper into status quo where how we truly feel deep in our souls is replaced with the pressure to be liked. Anyone seriously wanting to connect to their true self will need to recognize the social impairment of social media on the journey to heal. Taking a break while journeying through your discovery process may help with the road to recovery. There isn't instant gratification attached to this process. It will require patience and perseverance, and many days you won't see any tangible payoff, but you will definitely experience nirvana when you get to the other side.

The tools I learned aren't new, and I am not the author or originator of any of them, but I am surely an accomplished student who knows how to teach what I've learned. That's the CEO in me. From all that I have learned, I've put together a playbook that works for me. The tools are universally available for the willing and able, and I had to tailor and customize them to fit my needs and my particular set of issues, as I'm sure will be required by anybody taking this work seriously. And in that regard, like any lifelong learner and teacher, I am constantly adding to my tool kit.

CHAPTER 18

I have a vast library of books. I have logged countless hours of therapy and learning from teachers. I've been to seminars in person and online—and lots of college coursework. I've participated in or led sessions at church and other settings and heavily rely on prayer and meditation. So, given my experience studying the mind, spirit, and emotions, I dove in with both feet to uncover what was hidden deep inside my heart in order to unlearn what was toxic and to relearn what would heal me. I started at the beginning, which is where I encourage everyone to begin. As you read in the earlier chapters, my story got off track early in childhood. I had to reckon with my painful past in order to clear room for a beautiful future.

Not all therapists are created equal. Many will set up a codependent relationship without even recognizing it. Look for more than education and experience; look for someone that is interested in helping you heal. That will require you interviewing more than one until you find the person that matches your need to pursue wholeness. Like pastors, therapists are people too often with challenges and struggles of their own. The title doesn't qualify them to usher you to the next level. Only chemistry and an understanding of where you're trying to go will do that. The first question you should be asking is if he or she is living inside their truth. When you think you've found the right one, then you ask the second question of how he or she found that truth. You will know you are in the right place when that person tells you they know exactly the travails of the journey and that it's up to you to do the work. Some will only treat the symptoms, and those are the ones that won't help you get to your place of depth. Be focused, and hold the therapist accountable to the work you are showing up to do. They can guide you, but the burden will be yours and yours alone.

Therapy will be slow and tedious, but it shouldn't take long to start touching on the core issues. You need to be willing to be vulnerable and trust the process. Otherwise, don't waste your time and money. Don't worry about being judged or ridiculed; they are trained professionals who've heard it all. You will only get out of it what you invest. If you are trying to get to the truth, you must bear it all and leave it all on the floor, crying, kicking, and screaming. A good effective therapist will be expensive and in-demand, which is par for the course. Just don't forget, therapy is the huddle, and the work begins once you leave your sessions. Your growth will happen as you apply what you are learning between sessions, and it should be supplemented with a bunch of other tools. I will cover some of the main tools that have worked for me.

CHAPTER 19

When we pry open doors that have been closed for a long time, we must be prepared for what awaits us on the other side. This preparation is rooted in understanding that we are not in control of what we find, but we surely can control how we respond once we find it. It's setting our mind and emotions into a receiving place. This is critical, because the goal is to heal, and we can't heal if we are not willing to be open to all the mess, dirt, junk, and brokenness that may surface.

Yes, our emotions will be activated, but it is the mind that will determine how successfully or not we can navigate those emotions. For me, I had to embrace memories and experiences from my childhood I didn't have consciousness of. I needed to understand the tragic truths of my family legacy that led to so much chaos and dysfunction. I had to reckon with how all of these events led me to continue to perpetuate a legacy of dysfunction in my own life. Then I had to make meaning of it all in order to dispatch the brokenness to make room for the goodness.

I had to come to grips with the justifications and lies I told myself as cover to coexist with my dysfunction. I had to forgive people who never apologized to me and forgive myself for the people who have forgiven me. It is unavoidable to protect against the shock and awe of it all when it feels overwhelming. But look at it this way, the price of freedom and wholeness is worth it. We are getting rid, once and for all, of the limitations on our ability to live our life fully. Women tell us the pain of childbirth is indescribable. It is said to be a pain like no other. Yet, the results of this pain brings about an indescribable love of new life, something that no parent can fully comprehend. The love that follows is as unbreakable as it gets. This is a poor attempt at an analogy to say in the end the investment of pain will bring about a new life you were literally born to dream and live.

What we learn in therapy should be supplemented by reading. You should not finish a session without asking the therapist for literature so you can go deeper into the subject matter. Remember, you are pursuing your truth, and this is not a passive exercise. This isn't about sitting on the couch once a week in a room to talk about your problems. This is a journey that you need to actively participate in. Fifty minutes once or twice a month talking about it isn't going to be enough to get you there. You need to develop your own primary knowledge of the concepts and theories yourself. This also serves as an accountability measure for your therapy. Be up front and let your therapist know you will be an active participant in your healing, and in between sessions you will dedicate yourself to study. Make sure your therapist comes with a ready reading list that will allow you to go deeper.

I have found that reading what I'm discussing allowed me grip and grasp my confusion, pain, and curiosities in ways that required a slower, deeper process of reflection. It was great using the conversation to open my heart and mind to an area we needed to explore, but we sometimes only scraped the surface. There is a value in starting, keeping, and building momentum, and that's what reading allowed me to do. If I had to constantly start and stop waiting for the next session to pick up where we left off, I'd in some ways take two steps forward and one step back, but reading between sessions allowed me to keep moving forward with momentum. By the next session, I had positioned myself for advancement.

Getting the content nowadays isn't limited to books. YouTube has a treasure chest of content that I have found outstanding. I could read a book about attachment theory, and then find Ted Talks and other conversations, speeches, podcasts, and seminars I could watch and listen to. It is vital to have good study habits, and you should study at your own pace. This entire process is about you, so settle in and get comfortable being a student.

If you look at your healing journey as nothing more than an education, you will set yourself for success. Part of any educational journey is being confronted with information that will challenge conventional wisdom. Not everything you read or discuss will apply to you, and you will not agree with everything you read or discuss. Push back when it doesn't feel right, but embrace when it feels uncomfortable. During this journey, you will need to stand firm on some of your core convictions if they truly serve your higher calling, but be comfortable being uncomfortable as you shed habits, customs, and ideology that haven't served your best interest.

If you follow this advice, you will find yourself getting revelations and breakthroughs when you least expect it. Several years ago, while taking a long walk and listening to one of the many podcasts I follow, a giant light bulb turned on. I realized my perspective and approach were wrong for my particular set of needs. In therapy, we were stuck working through some emotional trauma. As conventional wisdom dictated, we were looking at some of my unhealthy emotional responses and trying to replace them with healthier ways to respond to things like abandonment and feeling unloved. I was looking for an emotional cure but began to understand there was no cure for fixing my emotional trauma because I was looking at it the wrong way. I had been living a life of habits, not trauma. Certain habits that were controlling me had been formed because of my trauma. That's when I needed a shift in focus. I stopped looking at the emotional trauma and started paying attention to the habits I maintained as a result of some previous emotional trauma. I had been stuck here for a while and couldn't figure out why my progress was stalled. I had already worked through the emotional trauma, but it felt like the trauma held certain parts of me in a dysfunctional space, and in that moment, that's when the magic happened. If I focused on habits, I could change my life.

CHAPTER 20

The very first habit I needed to examine and shift was how I thought. My thinking habits were the single greatest influence over my emotions, so that's where I began. I needed to answer the question "what did I think about myself and the world around me?" So, I committed myself to understanding my mind.

I heard neuroscientist Dr. Joe Dispenza say that 95 percent of people, by the time we are thirty-five years old, are merely a set of memorized behaviors and emotional reactions that unconsciously create an identity. Literally, only five percent of your mind is conscious and plugged into reality. That five percent is what we actively control, although we feel like we are controlling 100 percent. So, we are literally fighting a losing battle of controlling our lives, since 95 percent of our mind is in charge subconsciously. Joyce Meyer states in *The Battlefield of the Mind* that the only way we can truly heal and change ourselves is to rewire our thought patterns.

> *I was exhilarated by the new realization that I could change the character of my life by changing my beliefs. I was instantly energized because I realized that there was a science-based path that would take me from my job as a perennial "victim" to my new position as "co-creator" of my destiny. (Prologue, xv)—Bruce H. Lipton PhD*

Therapy would open me up. Reading and other studying in between sessions would sustain momentum and allow for deeper revelation, but the ultimate shift was changing my thinking. It mattered not if I was full of new learned ideas and hopes if my old thought patterns were running the show. The cement

90

to hold it all together was the mind itself. I learned that changing my thinking was the gateway to a new reality. My unconscious mind was the battlefield, and excuses were the enemy of change. Making excuses and justifying my behavior worked to counteract the new thinking patterns I was trying to instill, and thus worked to anchor me to old thoughts and behaviors.

The work I was doing daily was learning to rethink. The habits that kept me in my old thinking pattern persistently tried to overtake any new thoughts before they could take hold. It looked like this: I'd read a new book that left me feeling hopeful; I'd listen to a seminar that inspired me; I'd talk to a therapist that made me feel strong and courageous; I'd attend church or listen to a sermon that reinvigorated my ability to have faith and to feel like more than a conqueror. Overnight, my emotions would just revert back. My thinking would resume its usual, negative patterns.

Old patterns are indeed hard to break unless you look at your behaviors in their entirety. For me, the enemy within that always managed to steal my momentum was "justification." Somewhere along the way, right before I made a choice to do something that wasn't in line with my new way of living and thinking, I had to give myself permission to do so. When you're in flight-or-fight mode, it's easy to fall into character to survive. You don't have to think about it, you just do it, and after a while, it just becomes natural. But when you are actively working to break those habits, you have to go slow and work even harder because doing things differently doesn't feel natural at first. Making healthy choices after years of acting on unhealthy circumstances requires focused attention, just as breaking years of bad eating habits.

But the justification cut both ways. I was now responsible for my choices and was aware of the difference between healthy and unhealthy choices, and still sometimes I found myself choosing the latter. But now that I was aware, I had to look at it and accept the hard truth. If I lied, it was because I didn't want to hurt the person I lied to. If I slept with someone I wasn't supposed to sleep with, it was because I was deserving of having my needs met because they weren't being met elsewhere. If I wasn't meeting my exercise goals, it was because I worked long hours and deserved to rest. If I was eating something unhealthy, it was because you only live once, and I'm entitled to indulge every now and then.

Regardless of the justification or excuse, I rationalized my way to choices that weren't in keeping with covenants, promises, and commitments I made to myself and others. I'm not talking about overcommitting, which I also had a habit of doing. I'm talking about having failures in my integrity. The reasons, whatever they were, felt just as real as the truth. As a result of having iron-clad excuses to justify my behavior, I never allowed myself to see or feel the impact of these breaches in integrity. However, they were breaches nonetheless, and no matter how sound my arguments were to myself, giving me permission to act, my behaviors were still destructive. As long as I kept making justifications, I could never reach the place of promise I desired and was created to reach. So, I threw justification and excuses out the window and fought my way to new thinking patterns. No longer were the days when I took something bad and convinced myself it was okay. I now rooted myself into serving my truth, which in turn served my purpose, which in turn landed me at my destiny.

CHAPTER 21

There is honor among thieves, but the thief is still living a life of crime. If I was ever going to get to my purpose-driven life of destiny, I had to put in more work to adopt another aspect of integrity, which was morality. Holding morality next to truth no matter how I was conditioned was the only way to embrace the realness of integrity. As long as I was able to justify my behavior or orchestrate circumstances and relationships to serve my self interest, I wasn't winning. In order to take the next step in my progress, I had to stare at the truth and uncover the true power of living within it.

In his book *Immortal Diamond*, Richard Rohr talks about the true self and the false self.

> *Your egoic false self is who you think you are, but your thinking does not make it true. Your false self is a social and mental construct to get you started on your life journey. It is a set of agreements between you and your parents, your family, your school chums, your partner or spouse, your culture, and your religion. It is your "container." It is largely defined in distinction from others, precisely as your separate and unique self. It is probably necessary to get started, but it becomes problematic when you stop there and spend the rest of your life promoting and protecting it. Your soul, your True Self, your deepest identity, your unique blueprint—is who we were created to be before we were born.*

I had so many challenges to overcome my whole life, that hiding was all I could do to survive. I decided that the appearance of success was in fact success. An entire new world opened for me once I made the conscious decision to identify the sources of my emotions and the ways I reacted to them. To understand the behavioral patterns carried over from generations in my family and to peel the layers I had created and reveal my true self, pains and all. Unlike the pain of the past, this pain was healthy pain, like a cut healing under a bandage. This pain was the agony of no longer being who I thought I was, yet nowhere near who I was destined to be. I was entering a new realm, what St. John of the Cross called "the dark night of the soul." I had to go back to the place in which my story began writing itself. I had to go down into the hollow cavern of my past and see what had been written about me on those walls–all the good, the bad, and the ugly. And yet from there, surrounded by all that stuff set in the stone, I could see the faint and distant light, my truth, calling me.

I had a choice: stay inside the darkness, ruled by the history that had been written for me, or move toward the light.

I saw all my trauma, shame and dysfunction laid bare. I saw my dirty little and big secrets, mistakes, and failures. I saw my accumulated childhood scars and adult heartbreak. It was really too much to bear, too much to process. It was embarrassing and messy and confusing. I didn't want this awful truth about me to rule my future, but the journey forward was hard.

Up to this point in my life, I always thought vulnerability was a bad thing, that it makes you weak. I was wrong. Being vulnerable to my past created an opening for truth. The more I paid attention to the history written on the wall, the more I blessed the realness and authenticity of my life story. I had lived through—suffered in some cases—and survived all of that trauma and damage. Mask or no mask, I had survived. This was my life and my story, and it was real. The more I embraced the fact that stuff did happen to me and that I was responsible for my decisions, the more I realized that who I was and who I am supposed to be is so much more than stories from the past.

My truth had always been with me. It was me and I was it. My true self is my vulnerable self, and my vulnerable self is my power. The ability to be vulnerable allows me the freedom not to be perfect, but to be brave. To be able to say no to what wasn't in my best interest and to say yes to things that nourished and inspired my soul. It was forgiving those that hurt me and forgiving myself for hurting others. It was embracing that yesterday will never manifest, tomorrow may never come, and today is the opportunity to live within my gifts and talents.

Owning my story and embracing the truth of who I am allowed me to see the future I am supposed to be living. By reconnecting to the original past, I connected to the original future. I didn't need to be perfect anymore. Instead, I wanted peace, freedom, and joy. Peace knowing that my story is as important as any other person's. Freedom knowing that my life and everything it has ever been is a work of art. Joy knowing that loving God and loving myself are all I ever needed to thrive no matter my bank account, contact list, or popularity.

CHAPTER 22

Vulnerability is defined by *Merriam-Webster* as: easily hurt or harmed physically, mentally or emotionally. Brené Brown PhD, LMSW, defines it as "uncertainty, risk and emotional exposure." I'm going to add the word "fear" to these definitions. From my personal experience, and from the many people I've talked to over the years about sensitive situations in their lives, fear is always there. We're afraid people will change how they feel about us if they knew our dirty little secrets. Whether it is a spouse who stepped outside of the marriage, a person struggling with an addiction, a victim of molestation or any other difficult experience, mistake or regrets, we'd rather hide and conceal than embrace and understand.

We prefer to hide our sexual identity, history of domestic violence, the burden of massive debt. We don't talk about bad grades, a demotion at work, or if we're an ex-convict. These and so many other situations that we've endured, created, or witnessed we work to keep secret. We tuck this history away in our closet because we believe if we can forget or erase the past, we will be protected emotionally, physically, and mentally.

We all have a story, and each of our stories has peaks and valleys. I do not know anyone with a perfect story, without any challenges to overcome. Oftentimes, those that present a perfect picture to the world are usually the ones with the most to hide. We hide our stories and truths to hold onto our station in life, reputation, and perceived love and support from people.

I believed if my story was perfect, then I would be viewed as perfect. I wanted to be viewed as perfect because my truth was a mess. If people found out about my past or current struggles, I feared they might choose to use that information against me or to take advantage of me, to inflict harm or take something away from me. I perceived they wielded this power, so I freely handed it over to them.

When I stopped to look deeper at this dynamic, instead of being led impulsively by emotion, I was able to separate fact from fiction. The fact is that those that truly loved me unconditionally were there to support me and help me navigate my confusion and struggles. They held my hand through the healing because they loved me. Those that didn't love me weren't going to be there for me regardless, so there was no need to continue to invest in people that weren't rooting for my success anyway. I had to allow my fear of being judged to melt away so that I could get to what mattered most: embracing who I was, flaws and all, and standing firm in my story, including all the bad stuff I endured.

Once I was able to stand in my story, I learned that I wasn't afraid of people. All this time, I was afraid of myself. Although I have always tried to be a good person, I have hurt people from my actions in the past. I've also suffered at the hands of others that left me wounded. Whether I was the one doing it or having it done to me, I believed sharing my baggage would set the stage for people to judge me, fire me, avoid me, ostracize me, and simply change how they treated me.

I began to crave the freedom and peace that could only come from surrendering to the demons of old and harkening to the better angels of tomorrow. In therapy, we discussed my desire to be me. The books I was reading told stories of others that somehow managed to live a life of purpose. At first I was ashamed of all the hurt and regret I held onto, but the longer I stared, the more familiar I became with my own eyes. I was able to look into my soul and see me.

I gave myself permission to love the man I saw in the mirror. What started as a stare, then turned to tears and finally a small smile. I didn't need anyone's permission. I didn't need anyone's praise. I just needed to trust I was created for more. That my past didn't equal my future. In order to take that first step, I needed to start sharing my story. I told the men at church who I was and what I'd survived.

I shared with them everything: the domestic violence growing up, being molested by my babysitter, cheating on women I was with, and so much more. I had decided that if they all turned on me so be it, but at least I'd be free. I embraced vulnerability and stared down judgment. I was no longer held back by fear or worried about losing the wrong people. I talked and talked and talked, and when I was done, silence fell over the group.

Then something miraculous happened. Man after man began to share things that held him prisoner. They told of their mistakes and regrets and failures. There wasn't a dry eye in the group. Then, one by one, they turned to me and thanked me. In laying myself bare, I had given them permission to put down the weight of hell and pick up the promise of life. They said the courage and bravery that I had shown freed them to be brave and courageous. And just like that, I was a free man.

There were other people outside this setting that I shared my story with. Some pulled away, and others moved closer to me. Funny thing is, though, that any of the relationships I no longer had as a result of my past weren't real in the first place. I just never had a reason to take inventory of them. In the end, I gained lifelong, true friendships and shed people that didn't mean me any good in the first place. The fear of being judged was a fear that, like my fear of vulnerability, only held me back. My dirty little secrets aren't dirty at all, and they're not secrets. They're my history. I am the sum total of my lived experiences, thinking, relationships, and behaviors. To minimize any one of these is to diminish myself, and I had had enough of that. To diminish myself was a form of self-rejection, and what's the point of rejecting any part of who I am if I'm stuck with being who I am for the rest of my natural days? Being free to embrace my entire life publicly and openly is one of the reasons I'm able to thrive in life today.

CHAPTER 23

Today I am a new man. I still struggle. I still find myself picking at old wounds. I still hear the demons trying to lure me back to a place of darkness. But now I understand why, and I have the tools to pull myself through. I can look back and see how I allowed my reactions to turn into personality traits, and because of this, I am now able to prevent it. In the past, if something bad happened to me, I would internalize it. If I held onto that feeling for a while, it turned into a bad mood. If I did nothing to change my mood and I held on longer to the negative energy, it became a temperament. If I remained in this temperament without intervention, eventually over a prolonged period of time it turned into a personality trait. Without realizing it, I allowed that negative energy to change me, which was the root of my dysfunctional behavior.

Having embraced my truth, giving myself permission to be vulnerable and shedding the fear of being judged, in order to sustain this progress and hold onto wholeness, I needed to learn how to navigate contrary winds whenever they should blow, lest I find myself right back to square one holding onto negative intersections in my life. Earlier I talked about the mind and how I had to reset my thought patterns. No new way of thinking, no new life. However, being able to hold onto healthy thought patterns in the face of adversity was just as critical as building the new thought patterns in the first place.

It's one thing to make all of the decisions I made to rid myself of my mask and to start living from a place of purpose. It's something entirely different to be able to hold onto those changes after years and years of being programmed to think a certain way. With the majority of my actions (approximately 95 percent on average) being driven by my subconscious, to cement lasting change required, and still requires, me to routinely access and write on my subconscious mind the positive thoughts and behaviors that help move me closer to my destiny.

Setting goals and achieving them with sheer willpower alone I thought was enough to get the job done. Stopping old habits and starting new ones would require more than emotional inspiration and determination. I had to re-engineer my patterns to get to the result I wanted. I wanted internal joy and peace. I wanted to live from a place of purpose. I wanted to fully utilize my gifts, talents, and calling—and I wanted all of these things now.

So, I began to cement new habits into my daily life that would anchor my behavior and thought patterns and drive me towards achieving my goals, even if in small incremental levels. The structure of my mornings became the canvas in which I could write my story for the day. The beginning of the day is where I won the battle before even stepping a foot outside my door.

Science tells us that the first ten to thirty minutes after we wake up in the morning our brain waves are moving slow enough for us to write on our subconscious. This is called the alpha phase. During alpha, we have a unique opportunity and gift to reprogram some of that 95 percent. I keep my iPad on my nightstand and ready set to content that will grow my mind. As soon as I notice I'm awake, I reach over and hit play. I've been doing this for several years now, and the amount of growth and learning I've done during that brief window is more intense and impactful than all my MBA courses combined.

The next thing I do is drink water and read a devotional. Most mornings, I'll exercise and meditate as well. All this before I check texts, email, read news, social media, or open my mouth. I've learned to feed my mind, heart, and soul before I even speak a word. By the time my day is ready to start, I'm operating at such a high frequency of peace and productivity, I'm virtually ready for anything.

What does all of this have to do with sustaining my new station? Everything. I have to be intentional about cultivating my day. The world and the people in it are constantly trying to pull me in all sorts of directions. As the poem "Invictus" says, "I am the master of my fate, the captain of my soul." Having a plan for the plan keeps me moving forward, focused, and living deep inside my purpose.

I used to be one of those people that would constantly set goals and either forget about them or abandon them. I noticed every so often I would come back to resetting those same goals year after year. I was sincere about my goals, and at the times I set them, you better not have bet against me. Then life would happen, conditioning would set in, and I was back to drifting.

Now that I have taken writing onto my subconscious seriously, I have no problems breaking bad habits and sustaining new ones, which allows me to set and keep the goals I set.

CHAPTER 24

I've learned to trust my gut. This wasn't always the case, because I used to be blinded by my dysfunction, and I did what a lot of people do, which was resign myself to the fact that whatever happened happened. I was socially conditioned to maintain the status quo. Don't quit a good-paying job. Don't get out of a dysfunctional, codependent marriage. Don't risk your small fortune starting a new company because it was too risky. Don't think differently because nobody in the pack is stronger than the individual. I could go on and on about how much value I was taught to place on conformity, which always came at the expense of freedom. I was taught freedom was selfish and bad for families and children. That freedom was too risky and not worth losing everything. That good enough was just that, enough.

All those years leading up to my panic at the White House, I didn't trust my gut because it didn't align with my conditioning. But once I found a way to rework my way of thinking, I heard the fullness of what my gut was saying to me. It was always the same thing. It said, "Go in the direction I'm telling you to go and don't look back." But change is scary, and it can hurt because it sometimes requires changing some of the people closest to us.

I remember when I first began letting people know I was going through a divorce. I was embarrassed and worried about being judged. It was difficult, and I felt in many ways I had failed. What I had presented was the perfect picture to the world. I had all the trappings of success, and yet it wasn't healthy for my soul or purpose or calling. People would also ask me how my family was doing. The first few times I would respond with the proverbial "fine," which is the universal socially acceptable way to hide our mess when things are far from fine. It's just easier to lie and avoid vulnerability and not risk being exposed. Not only was I lying, but the lie was a barrier to my truth. Why? Because being honest about my struggle was not something that would impress people. I grew to realize that feeling embarrassed was a sign of progress and is an emotion I should gladly and boldly endure. So, now I keep it totally real if someone asks, and that's that.

Being able to speak my truth and absorb how others felt about it would push me deeper into my truth. It was positive feedback that I was on the correct path and moving forward. I decided that embarrassment was a badge of honor and that my feeling of embarrassment was how freedom felt. After I had this revelation, I never again dodged the question of how my family was doing. I'd say, "I'm going through a divorce," and wait for a reaction or response. Most of the time, I'd get the standard "I'm sorry to hear that," and I'd ask, "Why?" They didn't know why they were sorry, but it was a conditioned response. Several times, in fact, we'd end up talking about their relationship because I was open about my status.

Whether it was my divorce, buying out my business partners who were no longer good fits for my professional future, or moving to a church that fed my soul, I was no longer bound by what others thought. I was more determined to live a life completely draped in my truth, even if it meant people would get upset and/or disagree with me. Most of the time, people became inspired by my decisions and ability to live in my truth. It also opened up the opportunity for me to discuss the masks that they'd constructed.

Change doesn't have to be ugly, but sometimes it is. I've had my trials as I've navigated new doors to walk through and old doors to shut. I used to think it was all always supposed to be "all good," that the choices I made were about happiness. I've learned that happiness comes from external factors, but joy comes from the trusted peace from within. I had to surrender all the things that I thought would make me happy in order to embrace the tough decisions and transitions that brought me joy.

I can honestly say that no matter how hard things get or how tough it is sometimes to endure challenges, I've never once lost my joy, even on down days. I am blessed to have the full range of emotions, from bitter to sweet and everything in between, and I allow them all to hold me when it's their turn. What I don't do is forget who I am and where I've been. I do not lose sight that when I lived in my mask I lived a life of fiction. Now that I'm living a life of truth, purpose, and destiny, all the struggles, pain, and suffering were a small price to pay for admission to the life I'm living, a life from which dreams are made.

I say seek the truth of your purpose over the approval of people every day of the week—and twice on Sunday.